Connecting
with the Arcturians

channeled by DAVID K. MILLER

Other Publications by
David K. Miller

Connecting
with
the Arcturians

channeled by DAVID K. MILLER

All text channeled by David K. Miller
Cover art and illustrations by Gudrun Miller
Transcribed by David and Gudrun Miller
Edited by Nan and Len Cooper
Text and chapter organization by Len Cooper
Photographs of David and Gudrun Miller by David Miller
First edition published by Planetary Heart Publications

ISBN-10: 1-891824-94-5
ISBN-13: 978-1-891824-94-4

Published and printed in the United States of America by:

PO Box 3540
Flagstaff, AZ 86003
800-450-0985
www.lighttechnology.com

Spiritual Galactic Consciousness

One With All Being—All Beings As One

We dedicate this second printing of Connecting with the Arcturians *to the over 1,200 starseeds worldwide who are currently members of the Arcturian project known as the groups of forty. These members are helping to support and bring down Arcturian fifth-dimensional energies to our beloved planet.*

I also wish to thank Melody O'Ryin Swanson, owner of Light Technology Publishing and the Sedona Journal of Emergence. *She has supported my Arcturian channeling for many years in her beautiful magazine,* The Sedona Journal of Emergence, *and she has now made it possible to reprint this book, which was originally published in 1998. The book has grown in popularity over the years, and the messages contained in these lectures seem more relevant now than ever before.*

In love and service,
David and Gudrun Miller,
Prescott, Arizona, 2011

CONTENTS

INTRODUCTION

We live in a rapidly changing world. The explosion of knowledge and technology is creating a strain on all current personal and institutional belief systems. Many of our old truths are in the process of rapid disintegration. Therefore, we are currently immersed in a major transition of human consciousness.

Transitions are always chaotic and unstable. But this particular transition is very profound because it affects all aspects of our perceived reality. We are being bombarded with new perspectives, new ideas, a new age, a new concept of God, new extraterrestrial neighbors, new prophecies, a new spirituality, new definitions, and a new personal and planetary identity.

Unfortunately, much of this new information is contradictory, confusing, and very difficult to integrate. We are being simultaneously exposed to so many new concepts that the usual human ability to process and integrate new knowledge is being short-circuited. More questions exist than answers, and the necessary details for intellectual understanding are not always presented.

For proper absorption, all new concepts must be released in their correct time. One cannot understand a higher view of reality until certain prerequisites of understanding have been met.

We have been working hard to reach this moment in time. We have been preparing ourselves for the unveiling of a greater picture, a higher understanding, a new, expanded perception of what is happening to us. We are ready to understand what our beloved Mother Earth is preparing to do. We are ready to perceive what is in front of us, not only as individuals, but as a race of beings.

The Arcturians give us a clear look into the fifth dimension. This new reality is much different than our current third-dimensional existence. In the fifth dimension, all things are manifested through focused thought. Everything is experienced as an energy pattern. Thus, the Arcturians refer to an object or a being as "an energy." All things can be healed through the balancing and distribution of different energies. Different energies have different attributes, similar to our atomic structures. The potential for creation is actually much greater when working with higher-frequency energies. Thus, the fifth dimension is more dynamic and expressive than the heavier, slower, third dimension. It is not limited by fixed atomic relationships.

Only on rare occasion does a book come along that contains the potential to change the consciousness of our entire planetary culture. Many have talked about the ascension process, but very few really understand what it means. Who is really out there? Where are we going? What are our choices? What has to be done to prepare for this event? Is everyone ascending to the same place? What happened to the fourth dimension? How can we understand the fifth dimension? What does it feel like? How does it operate? What are fifth-dimensional beings like? How do they live?

This book explains all of these questions in a way that we can easily understand. It explains what our relationships are to known extraterrestrial groups, and what they are doing to help the Earth and her people in this crucial galactic moment in time. It explains how we can raise our vibration now, and begin the process of integrating higher dimensional energies into our third-dimensional world.

The Arcturians have also given us a crucial focus for the acceleration of world consciousness. They have presented the concept of group ascension through the creation of groups of forty. They have also presented the concept of the Sacred Triangle, a method for the integration and unification of spiritual and religious thought on the planet Earth.

All those who read this book will feel the presence of fifth-dimensional energy within their being. You will be able to truly experience a view of fifth-dimensional awareness. This will profoundly effect your ability to expand your own perception of reality and help you to actively participate in the personal and planetary ascension that has already begun.

Len Cooper
Planetary Heart Publications

CHAPTER 1

WE ARE THE ARCTURIANS

We are the Arcturians, and I am Juliano, one of the commanders of the contingent that is overseeing the Earth connection. We have a very strong interest in the Earth, for we view ourselves as the midwives of your spiritual birth into the fifth dimension. You would not expect a human baby to be born into the third dimension without assistance to both the mother and the baby. Therefore, we have been designated as powerful helpers for you in your birthing process. We are like a magnet that is attracting your spiritual energy into the higher realms.

Please understand how important it is for you to have this magnetic attraction. There are many distortions and diversions on your third dimension. We know that you experience difficulty when you are trying to concentrate. We are experts on focusing energy into the higher spiritual realms. Our working with you is going to foster and accelerate your development in a way that will help you to move into the fifth dimension in a comfortable and smooth fashion. Thus, we view our coming together as part of your ascension process.

Many of you have multiple, past life connections with different star systems, such as the Pleiades, and other galactic systems that you are not consciously aware of in your Earth knowledge base. I remind you that you connect to the other star systems through the Arcturian stargate—through us. We are loving beings, serving the highest wisdom. We do not interfere but only bring you to these planes as your assistants and guides.

It is important for you to learn how to interact with the higher dimensions and how to become more proficient at interfacing with other planetary beings who are in alignment with the goals of your development. This is most important when you are experiencing what you call extraterrestrial beings, for you must be very careful that you align with those who understand and support your chosen path of evolutionary development.

You may think of us as highly developed spiritual beings from the fifth dimension who are assisting the Earth beings in their transition. We experienced our own third-dimensional shift, our own ascension, a very long time ago. We have evolved to a higher state of consciousness, a state that many of you very much admire and wish to participate in. This state of consciousness has to do with the overcoming of primitive, basic instincts, and the moving to a higher frequency that will allow you to exist in your lightbodies.

This really is the purpose of your evolutionary path on the Earth. You wish to leave the physical and go into the light. What is meant by "go into the light"? It is your ability to be in your lightbody, free of the physical constraints of the Earth, free of the need for the very contracted aspects of your life, those aspects that have to do with the finiteness of the conception of your existence.

Not only have we worked with many starseeds, but we have also seen many planets go through evolutionary shifts. It is of great interest to us to observe the Earth and the planetary shift that she is currently experiencing. Never has there been as much assistance available to a planet as there is now to the Earth. You need to know of the caring and concern that many higher beings have for the Earth, and you need to know that they are watching over you. They are also participating in the Earth evolution and her new birth. The Earth is literally being "born again." There is a continuous death and rebirth cycle in the universe. The Earth is going through a birthing process, and you are at the cusp of this evolutionary shift.

THE ARCTURIAN TRANSMISSIONS

We want to discuss with you the nature of our transmissions. First of all, we are studying you carefully, as well as helping you. We are studying your unfoldment as planetary beings. We are studying your resistance, your densities, and your blocks to the higher levels, including your acceptance of our existence. Part of this resistance focuses on your cultural upbringing, and your insistence in the educational process on logical understanding. On the one hand, this has been a major advancement. On the other hand, it has led you to many solid walls in your spiritual development as galactic beings.

We need to remind you of your abilities to transform and activate through light. We can reach you through speech, but part of our major message is also an energy exchange. As we speak, our ships in the fifth dimension are centered over you. Those who are hearing these words and reading these pages, know that you can expand your awareness to the fifth dimension. Know that the light from us and our ships can reach you. Do not be afraid to activate yourselves. You have sought us out because you have sensed a presence from another part of the galaxy within you.

Think of the excitement you will feel when you acknowledge that you exist in a galaxy in which you have opportunities to interact with countless other beings and entities. Just open up to that possibility. When you do, then you can receive transmissions from us.

Our transmissions are on a higher frequency that is still immeasurable by your instrumentation. When receiving us, there is a slight beeping sound that comes into your auric field. This activates special electromagnetic receptors in your cellular structure, enabling you to receive our thoughts. It helps you to "let go" in order to receive these messages. Then you can translate them into your language.

We have learned your language, and we have studied your thought patterns. We are familiar with your methods of deduction and induction. We have studied your fears, your reactions, and your human aggressiveness that has been such a problem. Your jealousies, your hatreds—we have explored these through many of our contacts and observations. At times, with the permission of your higher selves, we have temporarily resided in your bodies so that we could go through days with you, or weeks, or even months when that was acceptable. We have observed you so that we could learn more about your emotional states. We have appreciated the opportunity to be with you for such periods of time.

In return, we have offered you the reverse: we have offered invitations to you to reside with us. You can come with us in spirit to our planet, or visit our ships. The reverse, however, has been more difficult, for many of you have not adequately prepared for a higher frequency existence. We have found that, for the most part, you are in need of deep healing. The experience of being on the Earth has been very traumatic for most of you, and it requires some recovery. We are more than willing to make our technology and thought patterns available to you for your healing.

One of our special gifts to you is our thought patterns. We have certain frequencies that can be made available to others. These thought frequencies are not necessarily transmitted in words, although there are sounds that can be voiced. When you are able to exist on our frequency, you can experience an expansion of your cells, an expansion into your lightbodies, your light consciousness and your galactic selves. Open your minds to the possibility of being on a new frequency. We will be providing different sounds that will help to activate you to this frequency. If you are reading these words, simply connect with us in your thoughts, and we will be open to working with you.

Just tuning in on our frequency will provide an upliftment and an expansion for you. Frequencies are waves that you can ride. Receive our frequency into your fields. Direct your consciousness to your auras now and be open to receiving the frequency of the Arcturians. We are peaceful and spiritual. We seek higher development and higher ethereal contact. We can help you transcend your lower vibrations. It is through our abilities to work with frequencies that we can achieve higher states of healing, spiritual consciousness, and technological development.

THE ARCTURIAN EARTH MISSION

The Arcturians have been connected with the Earth and the human race in varying capacities for the past 150,000 years. We have been very involved in the affairs of the planet Earth for the last 20,000 years. Some of us were here much earlier, but this is the active phase of our planetary involvement. We have had major contacts with you in your current historic period. We were involved with the Hebrews on Mount Sinai under the direction of Sananda and others. We have been overseeing some of the evolutionary changes that have occurred. Even more recently, we have been able to work with many of the Native Americans very directly. Now, we are again working closely with many of you as starseeds. Thus, you can see that we have a long-standing kinship with the human race.

At this time, we have great contact and involvement with the Earth because so many Arcturian starseeds are here. We work with the permission of, and in service to, your White Brotherhood/Sisterhood. We acknowledge Sananda to be the ascended master of your planet. The guidance that he offers you is from the highest galactic source. We interface with that knowledge, as well as with his work and his great love. We acknowledge all of your religious experiences, only wishing to bring you into the highest interface with spiritual light.

It is true that other space beings are coming to your planet continually for observation. Presently, some are interacting with you. We are interacting only with certain chosen people on a modified level, but we are seeking to create an awareness of our presence. This has been authorized by the highest sources in conjunction with your planetary evolution.

We have not been directly involved in human evolutionary changes or genetic restructuring. Those issues were left up to the Pleiadians and the Sirians. Other extraterrestrial groups have also done these things. We, however, function more in the role of teachers or overseers. We are here to help you graduate so that you can ascend into the stargate and move into the fifth-dimensional realm.

Our current Earth mission is a very broad base mission. It is a mission of love, spiritual evolvement, and learning. It is a mission of connection, and, more specifically, a mission of energy infusion. Ascension is a form of expansion. To expand, you need to hold more energy. This is a universal law. We can help you accelerate your mental, emotional, and physical systems through the process of energy infusion.

The Earth is experiencing an interdimensional transition. The locks on the third-dimensional realms are being loosened, not only for you, but for the Earth as well. This is allowing a tremendous infusion of energy to occur. If you focus your energy on higher beings, like ourselves, you can work effectively in this new energy. We are very pleased that we can now anchor fifth-dimensional energy even more deeply into your planetary system, and help the Earth in her ascension process.

With the onset of this increased energy and the openings into the higher dimensions, you need a focus. That is one of our missions to you—to provide a consistent, etherically pure, and high spiritual energy focus for you. We are providing a gateway for you to meet us, just as we have a gateway to the galaxy. This is our gift to you. We want this to be a group gateway, for we communicate and work as a group consciousness.

We want to help you raise your level of consciousness to a point where you can enter the dimensional corridors that are now opening. You can use these dimensional corridors to communicate and interact with us. We can train you to work in interdimensional spaces and project yourselves through the corridors to our ships and then to the Arcturian system. We can help you to project yourselves to the interdimensional temples located on the beautiful mountains of Arcturus.

It is also our mission to assist you in your purification. Come to us in your consciousness, and know that we will assist you to purify and to cleanse, so you can raise yourselves and your planet to a higher level. We know how to help you purify your thought patterns. We realized long ago that when you refine your thought patterns, you are well on the way toward your spiritual birth.

We are a spiritual race, and we communicate telepathically. We are specialists in bringing you the highest spiritual light and in utilizing healing chambers in order to provide assistance to you. We bring down a golden blue beam of light for you. This light is sprinkling very powerful rays that will enter your crown chakra. We personally greet each of you with this burst of energy. We recommend that you take this energy into your crown chakra and expand your consciousness even beyond your emerging awareness of the Arcturians.

THE ARCTURIAN SYSTEM

We have a different name for Arcturus. It is in a language you would not be able to understand, but what it means is "the star that gives light" in much the way you look at a mother who is providing life-giving nourishment. It is a well-seasoned star that has been our focus for many eons.

As you might expect, our years are not like your years. Our planet travels around the star Arcturus once every three hundred twenty-two Earth years. You can imagine the difference in time orientation. We live in a solar system that has fifteen planets, and each planet is in a different stage of development. Some planets exist solely in the third dimension. Others exist simultaneously in the fourth and fifth dimensions.

In the Arcturian system, we live predominantly without a gravity field. There is, however, a slight gravitational pull on our etheric presence. We are now overseeing an inhabited planet in our system that is third-dimensional like the Earth, but moving toward the fifth dimension. We are assisting those souls by helping them to reincarnate through the Earth system, and then use that energy to connect to an access point into the fifth dimension. Many Arcturian starseeds currently on Earth come from this planet.

THE ARCTURIAN CULTURE

We exist in a dimensional reality that is of a clarity that you cannot currently comprehend. The purity and the clarity on our planet would be very refreshing to you. You would immediately sense a personal purification upon initial contact with us. The extra baggage you carry on your third-dimensional world would be immediately eliminated.

We have no concerns about physical survival, security, retirement, pension, or even forms of primitive work. These matters are not included in our realm. We devote our time and space to spiritual life. This is not a life without pleasure, do not mistake that. We engage in music and in relationships. We engage in work, but it is not on the primitive level that your culture and society demands. The work is more suited to our individual desires and spiritual paths. This higher concept of work is something that you are now seeking.

We are very focused on the color blue. We focus on intermingling with other dimensions. The whole system of our civilization is based on a group of leaders who are deeply involved in thought projection. They help to maintain the structure of our civilization, its codes, its spiritual harmony, and unity. The foundation of the system is maintained through thought projection. This is the true work of our leaders. They are specially chosen, and they are trained to maintain the thought projections of our system. This allows others to engage in exploration. Our explorers know that they can return to our base of operation. When we travel interdimensionally, it is important that we take with us workers who will continue to connect with our base of operations through thought projections.

Thought projection requires a concentrated effort and an ability to be extremely focused. It is used by the Pleiadians and the Arcturians for the manifestation of objects and tools. We have special training centers that teach thought projection. The first step is to remove attachments, for you cannot do thought projection for personal gain or greed. That is one of the laws of the universe. If the ego is too involved in these projections, then the task becomes impossible. Teaching the principles of thought projection involves instilling the knowledge of how to use this tool wisely.

All beings, including humans, possess a particular frequency that allows us all to uniquely express ourselves in a mission. Your mission is a symbol and a significant sign of your starlight. We attune to that concept very early in our children's development, so that we can immediately provide the highest stimulation and direction for each child. We are not competitive, for we are trained to realize that each of us has a unique frequency, or purpose.

The Arcturians are a very peaceful race. We have not been involved in warfare for a very long time. We do have the ability to manifest in the third dimension. We have the ability to protect ourselves on our ships, but we are not engaged in anything that is even close to any form of conflict. If we encounter a problem, we can immediately dematerialize. Thus, any object that would be projected our way would simply go through us, and not cause us any harm. Many extraterrestrial civilizations have learned how to do this.

On Arcturus, we too experience the death of our form, but our passing is experienced in a much different sense. For it is not conceived as the end, but merely as a transitory state of our existence. Our Arcturian lives are only one of the many different multidimensional selves that is part of our complete being.

THE ARCTURIAN ENERGY LIBRARIES

As your electromagnetic energy fields vibrate at faster rate, your memories will be activated. Go to the libraries of Arcturus in your thoughts. The libraries will be a very comfortable place for you. These libraries are not like normal libraries on the Earth plane, where you go and read books. They are libraries of energy sources. So you must imagine that when you come into a library, you are remembering energy patterns and electromagnetic vibrations.

All of your historic religious masters have had exposure to, or elongated contact with extraterrestrial energies. Some did not even know that they were in contact with extraterrestrial sources. These contacts were experienced as gods or as angels speaking. All of your masters have reached the point of electromagnetic awareness that allowed them to experience a nonverbal, mystical energy. This is what you are moving to when you come into the Arcturian libraries.

The Eckankar is also very connected with Arcturian energy. The light vibration from the Eckankar is Arcturian in source. The light streams in the electromagnetic vibratory arrangements are very similar in frequency to the energy you will find in the Arcturian libraries. The Eck masters have freely come and worked in the Arcturian libraries. Many of them are accessing Arcturian energy from the libraries.

You are very verbal and very literal in your thinking processes, but you can also know and remember through an energy exchange. This has been the basis of the Eckankar process in its pure form, i.e., an energy exchange. This comes directly from the Arcturian spiritual schools where you are trained and taught through energy magnetism. Bring yourself to the point of allowing that process to occur within you.

FORM AND APPEARANCE

We will send you an image of our appearance. Do not use the Zeta Reticuli as a standard. You may picture a slender being that is a male. In your terminology, he is approximately five feet eleven inches tall, very slender, with flowing hair. He has a cape that comes down to the waist. His face is slender. He has large eyes, eyes that are twice the size of human eyes. His ears are relatively small and slender. His mouth is slender, with thin lips. Talking is not a high priority because we use thought transmission. He is very pleasant. Can you imagine that figure?

We are manifesting our presence to you. We will work through Gudrun for the drawing of the picture, and she will have all the necessary information and guidance. Perhaps this picture could be included with some of the writings, as many people are curious about us and we understand your desire to picture us more fully.

This is the best form for us to assume during a third-dimensional interactive state, but we can exist on many levels, and we can assume other forms. To come into this dimensional level, however, we have a specific form that we assume. Were you to meet us on another level, you would interact with us in another form. You would have no way of describing that other form in Earthly terminology.

You would not be able to relate to our pure form now, because you are still maintaining your physical presence. Your physical presence on the Earth requires a certain confinement of thought and energy. When you are able to break out of this confinement, you will know that you are also vibratory beings who do not need to be encased in physical bodies. You are currently evolving toward this perspective. This is also the perspective that is involved in ascension. You must realize that your physical bodies are not required for your continued existence. The goal is to become more wholly invested in your lightbody, or vibratory form.

You may question our physical structure and our apparent lack of physical strength. Because of our highly developed thought processes, we can use telekinesis and teleportation for moving ourselves and other objects. We do not need to use any form of physical exertion. Mental powers are so much more efficient! We do not need to create objects that are heavy. Our technology is advanced enough to make objects light and easily moveable with the mind.

You can even sense "thought movement" on Earth when you have light objects around, such as a feather or a piece of paper. When the wind blows you know the paper may move. Sometimes you can even encourage the wind to come and that will move the paper. Such an action is a beginning sign of telekinesis. If you are interested in developing your telekinesis skills as well as your telepathic skills, then we suggest you work on very light objects in the early stages. We will not guarantee your success. You have not been trained at an early age to engage in these processes the way that we have from childhood.

ARCTURIAN CONSCIOUSNESS

We are individual souls, but we constantly relate to our group soul. However, we relate to our group soul in a way that is not easily understood by you. You perceive coming into a group consciousness as giving up your individuality. However, coming into the group actually enhances your individuality. We are not advocating that there should be a mass giving up of individuality. We have individual souls, but we are so highly evolved that we are in touch with our group soul constantly.

THE ARCTURIANS

Juliano and Helio-ah stand in front of a very large space ship, but it is still more of a shuttle rather than a mother ship. The Arcturians gave quite a bit of detail about the image. They stated that the female, Helio-ah, is smaller and has feminine features as we know them. Her eyes are almond shaped, while Juliano's eyes are round. She has distinct eyebrows, while Juliano has none. Helio-ah wears pants with a slight flare as opposed to Juliano's more fitted pants. Both wear capes, and they display the symbol of the Sacred Triangle near their right shoulder. On their feet they wear shoes that form to the foot like a sock. They have only three digits on their hands and on their feet.

Their clothes are luminescent, and they are surrounded in a white-golden halo light. As I painted them, I felt their love and compassion guiding my hand. Juliano and Helio-ah are twin flames, and they complement each other well.

Gudrun Miller

We have gone beyond the ego boundaries you still experience. We have gone beyond even the physical dimensions you exist in, such as your body form. We have developed techniques for group souls, or extended families, as you have called them. You might think that our individual selves have been given over to the group self. This has occurred in some local galactic civilizations. The Zeta Reticuli have experienced an evolutionary lapse, a weakness in their chain. Because of their complete focus on the group, they have not been able to progress. They have lost too much of their individuality, and they have begun to lose their genetic vitality. Fortunately, we did not have this problem. We were able to encompass and integrate the needs of the individual with those of the group.

Please understand that, in our perception, we are a group energy, and we participate in group soul activity. You ask us if we are mental; the answer is yes, we are mental. We are communicating with you mentally. We are not channeling through what you would consider emotional responses. We believe you can access this emotional energy through your other great leaders such as Mother Mary or Sananda-Jesus. Our role is not necessarily to repeat that message of emotion for you, for there are others who are already bringing that vibration to you.

To assume that when a being is mental, he does not feel love or is not emotional, is not a view we adhere to. How can one exist in a mental framework without an emotional-body presence? We feel that mental energy is not necessarily an energy of detachment. From our perspective, as you rise on the mental plane, you become the observer and the object together, without losing either boundary. It is your philosophy that has perhaps led you to believe that you must give up one of them. Our message to you is that when you merge with your group soul, you are expanding rather than losing yourselves.

We have evolved far beyond the emotional problems that are so prevalent on the Earth. We have the ability to surpass all of the negative emotions that have been plaguing your planet. We know that many of you view us, the Arcturians, as predominantly mental beings. It is true that we wish to help you develop your mental bodies. Yes, we are very scientific beings, but we can also help you to clarify and purify your emotional bodies. Of course, we are not solely mental beings. We are very much attuned to your emotional life and to your emotional well-being.

THE ARCTURIAN ENERGY

The Arcturian energy can be described as a crystal light. We are devoted to spiritual enlightenment. We know that the goal of spiritual enlightenment has to do with gathering and holding more energy. Do not think of gathering more energy in terms of having more material possessions. It really involves multidimensional holographic energy inclusion. The energy that we are working with and teaching you about is an energy that comes from all directions. It comes not just from the top or just from the bottom, or the front or the back—it is a total energy. You are not just a front, nor are you just a back. Your soul knows no bounds; your monadic self has no up or down. Your monadic self has nothing in it that you can define in your spatial perspectives.

It is interesting that when you speak of the Mother-Father Creator energy, you often say that you cannot describe this energy. Your monadic self is also indescribable. We have to come into a consciousness that, as close as possible, has no boundaries. In your pure state, you are also limitless and holographic in nature.

We are evolving to that state of total merging into the monadic self. In the merging process, we have developed the ability to transmute our energy into other dimensions. We have developed the ability to travel interdimensionally, both to higher levels or lower levels. When we do that, we must create a portal or a corridor. By entering your dimension, which is much denser than ours, we actually create an opening because we are bringing in higher energy. The Earth desperately needs such energy infusions. Just by connecting with our consciousness, you are helping to stabilize the energy infusion that we are offering the Earth.

Because the Arcturian energy is a vibration that is very light, it is oriented toward a group uplifting. We are experts in working with groups. This is one of the reasons why Sananda has called upon us. We know that the group consciousness generates more energy for you. You can ride on that group energy to lift yourself up. We do not ask that you forego your individuality or your discernment. All we ask is that you come together in groups. Then you can access the group consciousness and the accompanying powerful energy surge. This group energy will help you to overcome minor blocks and detours in your personal ascension process.

The energy of the Arcturian connection is contagious. Most of you who are lightworkers wish to resonate with us. In truth, in other lifetimes, you have been seeking an Arcturian connection. We have been designated as the high energy portal for this sector of the galaxy. It is the sector, or portal, that many have striven to reach. We work with you now to bring you to the highest level of your intuitive possibilities. We know that there are many problems that confront you in the third-dimensional existence. Some of these are physical problems of health, some problems have to do with financial matters, and some problems concern your employment. No matter what level of problem that you are dealing with, remember that our energy remains connected to you.

The Arcturian energy is like a thread of light running through your existence and connecting with us. Do not lose your spiritual awareness because of any third-dimensional problems. These third-dimensional problems do not mean that you are being punished, or that you are somehow spiritually inferior. Different levels and kinds of energy accumulate on this dimension, and it requires a very sophisticated perceptual awareness to be able to dodge all the different densities on the Earth plane.

Eventually, one of the levels of densities will catch up with you. You will run into one. It is not to be viewed that you are not living up to your highest potential. But you can consider it an opportunity for you to infuse yourself with more spiritual light. You may request that the energy be stepped up if you wish to receive a higher infusion of Arcturian light. We will bring you as much light as possible that you can assimilate without losing consciousness or becoming overly burdened.

We cannot infuse you with too much light if you are not able to tolerate the light. If this infusion would make you throw off your commitments to the third-dimensional level, then this is not acceptable. We want you to be involved in your third-dimensional existence. We are not trying to prematurely remove you from what you are experiencing on Earth. We recognize in all of you that you wish to be taken from your third-dimensional existence. We know, for a fact, that if we were able to, or decided to, or were given permission to remove you, then all of you would leave.

Many of you would joyfully give up what you have, because you think you would not have to conclude your third-dimensional drama. However, we are also aware that these individual, third-dimensional dramas are important to you and to your soul. As much as you may be distraught about that, these third-dimensional dramas are, nevertheless, important to you.

When you are in touch with this powerful Arcturian frequency, it does transform you. The Arcturian energy allows you to receive much information from us, and it can act as a healing force for you as well. When you have this Arcturian frequency within you, it will become so second nature to you that you will to be able to easily magnify your spirituality. While those around you are becoming more confused and unable to even hold a candle, you will be able to hold a great spiritual light.

CHAPTER 2

A GREATER REALITY

We live in a created universe of vast proportions. There is a center of the universe, but it is not something we can easily describe to you. You would have to understand the concept of a center without a beginning and without an end. The time-space universe surrounds the nucleus, or central universe.

THE TIME-SPACE UNIVERSE

The time-space universe expands and contracts in huge cycles. The expansion phase of the present cycle is what you currently perceive as the Big Bang. It will be followed by what you might describe as the Big Crunch, where everything in timespace eventually contracts. From our perspective, experiencing the cosmological contraction would not cause one to contract as a spiritual being. Furthermore, during a contraction, it is possible to expand in a way that will move one right out of the time-space universe altogether.

Expansion and contraction are philosophical questions to which we have devoted considerable time. When the universe reaches the point where it ceases expanding, time will momentarily stop, and the universe will begin to contract. At that point the universe will have evolved so far that the beings on the outer edge will go into light and enter a new, non-time-space universe. This will be experienced as an ascension. The contraction reaches a specific point just as expansion reaches a point. At that inner edge when contraction reaches a certain point, beings will also transform and move into a new realm.

We are aware of several other universes that have gone through this cycle of expansion and contraction. Studying this universe and other universes leads us closer to an understanding of these concepts. We want to experience this cycle or process. We are also studying the null universe in much the same way you are studying black holes.

The black hole is a model for the outer edge of the universe. One can say that the most outer edge, the very point where there is no more, is like a black hole. In one conception of the black hole, when something enters, that object goes through a conduit that leads into another realm. Some have referred to this conduit as a wormhole. Now imagine this: surrounding the whole outer edge of the present universe is a type of huge black hole.

We are studying the outer edge of the universe, and we are moving toward the point where we can experience transitions into the other universes from that point. This is the study of cosmology, or the understanding of the universe. These are important concepts, because you are here on the Earth to experience these processes, and the understanding of the universal energy force. You want to gain as much knowledge and understanding of these processes as you can, because it relates to the transition on Earth. One of your missions in manifesting the consciousness and awareness on the third dimension is to study this cosmology.

The source of the Creator energy, the source of light, and the source of spirit can be found in the stars. It is the sun that activates all life on the Earth, and it is the sunlight, or starlight, that activates all life on all planets in the galaxy. Without stars, no life would exist. The suns and the stars are everywhere in the universe. You cannot look at them directly without special protective glasses. You can, however, receive their special spiritual gifts. This is one of the secrets of the Central Sun concept.

The Andromedans search for the Central Sun in each galaxy. There is one star in our galaxy that is the center of the galaxy, from which all other stars came. It was the first primal star. This galactic Central Sun is connected to all other Central Suns in the universe, including the immense Central Sun at the center of the universe. When you find this Central Sun, then you can connect to all the Central Sun energies throughout all of the galaxies. This is an overwhelmingly powerful energy.

A council of light has been formed on Arcturus whose members are specially trained for viewing our galactic Central Sun. We are able to identify the Central Sun area. There are high beings of light that come from that area, beings of the magnitude of Sananda-Jesus. He is a manifestation of the Creator energy of the Great Central Sun.

THE MILKY WAY GALAXY

The biggest challenge for those of us exploring the galaxy is to move toward the galactic core. This project is still under intense study, for there is much controversy regarding how to approach the galactic center. There is intense energy from the Creator in the core. Many who approach the core do not wish to leave, and therefore, many do not return.

We cannot really describe the galactic core because it is indescribable. It would not be correct to say that civilizations exist in the core, because then you would be talking about a structure that is simply not needed there. Those who go into the galactic core and do not return are not having a negative experience. As those beings return to the center, the galactic core is strengthened. It is not a loss if someone goes to the core and does not return. It is not a black hole where energy goes in and is never seen again.

Evolved beings like Sananda can go there and come back if they so choose. There are several beings on a level equal to that of Sananda who are also able to accomplish this task. Those who are able to do it are so highly evolved that they can take others to that place with them. But it is one thing to be taken there, and it is another to come back out. We are trying to develop ways to guarantee a return from the galactic core. We have a commitment to communicate the experience to others.

A galactic gravitational field is also generated by the Milky Way galaxy. A very subtle wave is being constantly emitted by the galaxy. We can ride this wave and travel through the dimensions. You can ride the waves of the seas by sailing. However, when you enter into interdimensional space, you can become aware of not only this galaxy as a whole and ride its energy waves, but you can go to other galaxies as well. In fact, this is the preferable way to go from one galaxy to the next. There are many different variations in the methods of riding the galactic gravitational field. Your scientists will soon discover the antigravity method of propulsion. You will then be able to leave the planet without the exertion of large amounts of energy by propulsion systems.

THE PHOTON BELT

The photon belt is a system of energy that is coming upon the Earth, but it is not going to be a disruptive energy as many have predicted. Rather, it is an energy of shifting, an energy that will allow you to personally experience the dimensional planetary shift of the Earth. Many of you will be able to use this new energy to heal all of your irregularities. Open your heart to this new energy from the galaxy. We want you all to know that even the stars are sending special energy to you. Know that the sky itself is going to open in a new way, and different levels of energy will be coming into the planet.

Different facets of cosmological study relate to time travel, the null zone, and other energies in solar systems. The null system has been described as a point in the photon belt. The null zone within the photon belt is like a wormhole within a black hole that can drastically accelerate consciousness and energy. The null zone has been described by others as a point though which you can move into and through another dimension. Null zones exist within wormholes throughout the whole sector of the Milky Way galaxy. We refer to the sector of the Milky Way Galaxy you are in as the Mu sector.

Your solar system will soon be inside the photon belt, and will be going through a null zone that resides within the belt. The null zone experience is a big factor in bringing many of the extraterrestrials to your local section of the galaxy at this time. One reason why many are coming here is to study how you go through these zones. Imagine that a world was going through a black hole—would you not want to study that? You would want to study how they went in and if they would come out. Your planetary process is going through something like a wormhole, which is creating a transition energy. You are in that process now and are witnessing it. We, and many others, are coming to study how that process affects you. This process will lead to an ascension for many on the planet Earth. It is with great curiosity that we come to study this transition.

There are places throughout the Mu sector where events similar to your planetary process are in effect. There are strips and zones of energy transformation throughout your Mu sector. Remember that you are part of a large galactic sector. Other areas of the galaxy are also going through a transformation. The Milky Way galaxy is going through a transformation on a gigantic scale. You and the Earth are going through a transformation that is physically related to the energy that you call the photon belt. On a grander scale, parts of the galaxy are also moving through massive photon systems and thereby creating a transformation in entire galactic systems.

This point in galactic history, which you are experiencing as ascension and transformation, is reflecting a higher power of the entire galaxy. The Milky Way galaxy is reaching a point of mutuality of awareness as she comes into a new alignment with the Andromeda system. Eventually there will be a point of merging of these two galaxies. The Milky Way and the Andromeda galaxy will become a unified system. This represents a higher path of evolution in the galactic corridors.

THE SEEDING OF LIFE IN THE GALAXY

We have been exploring the entry of life into the galaxy. We know that life has been transported to different areas. There are many different interpretations of how life originated on the planet Earth. We know that you are curious to find the "right" answer. Life forms have been brought into this galaxy. The Arcturus system and your solar system are both close to the outer edge of the Milky Way galaxy. Life has been seeded from the inner levels to the outer levels of the galaxy. Many inner galactic systems and inner galactic species have been in existence for eons. Picture the entire universe as originating from a central location, and bringing life out to the outer levels. Life has been seeded from galaxy to galaxy, as well as from solar system to solar system.

Who was it that brought life to the Earth? Who is Yahweh? Who is Jehovah? You should know that He who is named cannot be the Creator. He who is named is not God but an aspect or even an entity of energy. The true Creator is not manifestable in the way of the spoken name. This is the truth of the *Kaballah*, but it is also the truth of the galactic energy. We, like the Pleiadians, share in the thirst and contact with this energy. We are searching for ways of expansion and ways to become closer to and more in alignment with this light.

Life was brought forth by Galactic Councils. It was decided to spread life throughout this sector of the galaxy. This was a conscious decision by a group of beings that you would consider to be gods in your level of understanding. There is a hierarchy of beings involved in the decisions of the galaxy. They are involved in the decisions having to do with the making of a planet, the making of a Messiah, and the Brotherhood and Sisterhood which oversees this entire operation.

The purest genetic "seed" is found in those beings who are closest to the Godhead energy. There is a search in the galaxies for that pure energy. However, rather than trying to find it, we are attempting to evolve our energy to become that pure light. We are moving steadily now in that direction of pure light. We ask that you would also focus your development on becoming pure lightbeings.

STARSEEDS

We want to talk to you about star communication and starseeds. Some of you are communicating with the stars, with the planet Saturn, and with our mother star, Arcturus, as you call her. Starseeds are those who are in communion with the galaxy and who have traveled throughout the galaxy in previous lifetimes. As you are going up your ladder of evolution and progressing in your karmic paths, you will finally reach a point where you can travel throughout the galaxy. You will become more aware of the stars and the dimensional shifts that occur.

Each section of the galaxy has a dimensional flavor and vibrational field that is unlike those of the other sections. There is an area in your galaxy that is considered the command post or the center of this sector of the galaxy. Some have been communicating with it through the Arcturian stargate.

Starseeds have lived many lifetimes in other worlds. Some have not been in higher dimensional worlds. Some have been in "equal dimensional places," but have been in a heightened state of evolution on that world. For the most part, the starseeds have come from this galaxy, and, in particular, your local section of the galaxy. Many of you have come from different planets in the local galactic sector, and you have chosen to reincarnate or to incarnate into the Earth planetary system at this time. You have deep interests and connections in planetary systems far beyond the solar system.

In order to withstand the different cosmic vibrations, you must be able to align your own vibrations with a higher frequency. Then you can travel freely to different sectors of the galaxy. Even if you could travel in your mental bodies through space, you would find that some areas you could not enter because of the different cosmic vibrations. This is why it is important to develop your sense of starseededness. By this we mean that if you are true starseeds, you can accommodate yourselves to vibrational shifts. You can accommodate different cosmic fields, even when they are in the etheric realms. When you are more earthbound, you have a harder time shifting. You will learn to adjust your vibration as you begin to travel.

It is perfectly acceptable to do out-of-body traveling through the star systems. You can move quickly with your mental body, especially when you are in areas like yours where you have direct access by means of your retinas. The resonation with your retinas is extremely important in activating areas of your brain that will unlock keys to help you vibrate with the star energy. This will advance your development as starseeds.

Starseeds, then, are those who are able to access cosmic vibrations and move through different sectors of the galaxy with ease. Moreover, starseeds are able to assimilate much information through direct channeling, such as you are now doing, and through visualizations. Starseeds are able to see interdimensionally. They are able to use their retinas to visualize, and thus, help manifest our ships in the third dimension. You are moving toward a time when you will be able to experience the physical manifestation of our ships. You must understand that the ships are not in your reality as a physical manifestation in the third dimension. When you see our ships, you are looking at a higher dimension that we refer to as the fourth and fifth dimension, areas you will be able to experience as you become more adept at being a starseed.

We are gaining more access through channels so that we can bring down specific energies that help you with group soul and starseed development. Remember that there are lightworkers and starseeds. The two are related, but different. You want to develop yourself as starseeds as well, not only as lightworkers or followers of Sananda and the Christ energy. Broaden yourself to become connected to the starseed energy and connected to beloved Ashtar, who has been in the forefront of interstellar communications. We salute him and his ongoing efforts.

There are many ways to experience enlightenment on Earth. Those who choose a path that is unrelated to starseeds may not go through the experience of relating to higher-dimensional beings. You who are reading these words are most likely starseeds, and you are enthusiastically seeking the light from the higher realms and extraterrestrials, which includes the Arcturians.

You are joining with us in moving closer to the Creator energy and closer to the universal oneness. As we move up, so do you. Our perspective is one of higher transformation, transcendence of incarnational cycles, and transcendence of the time-space dimensional system. This unification path will eventually enable you to also experience intergalactic and interuniversal energy.

OTHER ARCTURIAN ET RELATIONSHIPS

We have a strong interaction with the Pleiadeans. We work with them, and many exchanges have taken place where we have studied with them and they have studied with us. We are at a higher level in many ways than they are. This is a difficult subject to talk about. When we say "higher," you think of this as a contest. From our perspective, key spiritual and technological differences exist between the Arcturians and the Pleiadians. We ask that you do not take this in any way to be negative or judgmental statement.

Even though we have been invited to be helpers in the Earth's planetary ascension process, the Pleiadians will most likely make first contact. Since we are not of the same species as you, some would have more difficulty interacting with us rather than the Pleiadians, who are also of humanoid form.

You would find, for example, that we are more, from your perspective, androgynous as a being. You will find that the Pleiadeans have more of a traditional male-female sexuality. This is not a negative difference; it is simply a different evolutionary development. In some ways you would be more comfortable in a Pleiadian society. On the other hand, some of you are very fascinated by our higher evolutionary thoughts and our unique development. We do, however, come from different evolutionary streams.

We do not work directly with the Sirians. You have already been given a great deal of information about the Sirians and their role on Earth. We are very cautious in explaining their involvement on your planet. There has been both good and bad, in your Earth terms, bad meaning destructive, non-spiritual interactions with the Sirians and your planet. There has been an aspect of the Sirians that have dominated your planet. These Sirians have been involved in what you have called from your Biblical verses, the Nephilim, or the "Fallen Ones." Also, the Sirians continue to be involved with the planet that you have referred to as Nibiru. Other more positive Sirians have sought harmony and a higher evolutionary path.

The Sirians in some ways hold many keys to your problems. For example, it was the Sirian influence that allowed the development of nuclear technology on your planet. Likewise, it will be the Sirian influence that will help you clean up your nuclear wastes.

You have raised questions about the entity called Kryon, and about the suggested use of implants. We would say that you must evaluate the situation. The energy itself, the Kryon energy, is a well known powerful energy in the galaxy. We do not, however, work with this particular method that you call implants. We are aware that the release of negative karmic patterns is a high priority now. There could be some misunderstanding among your channels of how this release is done. We can tell you, from our experience, we do not recommend any type of implant for the release of any negative energy pattern.

It is fascinating for us to view the many different entities that are appearing to interact with you. We can only tell you that each of you has your particular path and your guides to work with. Some of you are very attracted to the Arcturians, and are working with us. We do not ask for your allegiance; we do not ask that you give up any part of yourself. We do not want you in any way to give up your free will. We simply offer our information that we make available to those of a higher and purer heart.

SPACE TRAVEL

We are highly advanced technologically. We are especially interested in mathematics, and the technology of time-space travel through mental imagery and antigravity acceleration. We engage in space travel by using the principles of dematerialization. There are technical matters involved as well, matters having to do with bringing large spacecrafts up to certain speeds. Traveling through space is not totally a mental phenomenon. There are scientific aspects of space travel that still need to be worked out.

The key to dimensional and interdimensional travel is thought projection. You project where you want to be and then the rest of you follows. We can help you to project yourselves to interdimensional space. Once you have achieved interdimensional and dimensional projection, you can continue traveling through the galaxy and even go to other parts of the universe. The ability to take along a ship, belongings and other objects requires a higher form of thought projection. Some have become aware of it through what you call telekinesis in which you can mentally move an object from one place to the next. This is a primitive example of the heightened skills you can perfect through thought projection.

Thought projection is involved in the propulsion of our ships. The ships spin like tops to gain centrifugal force. Then through thought projection we are able to move. As the ship moves in one direction, we focus our thinking in the counter direction. We then look for a portal in the space-time continuum. When we find that portal, we project our thoughts into that continuum and move through it quickly.

Portals, or energy corridors, have been created by beings higher than the Arcturians for the purpose of interdimensional travel. We also use portals to travel to different areas of the galaxy. Even though the primary force for this interdimensional travel is thought, a corridor still has to be established that will take us to another time-space coordinate. When we travel interdimensionally, we bring ourselves and our vessels to the portal, and then we accelerate our ship. This requires a very intense concentration far beyond what you are now able to do.

We have traveled throughout the Milky Way galaxy. There are approximately 2.4 billion stars in our galaxy. We certainly cannot say that we have visited every star, but we have traveled across the galaxy diagonally in several different directions. We have met and worked with the Council of Light from the galactic Central Sun. We are very focused now on bringing the energy and light consciousness from the inner galaxy to the outer areas of the galaxy where your solar system resides.

We also have traveled intergalactically. We have spent much time in the Andromedan galactic system. We have traveled to at least ten other galaxies, each having its own different developmental aspect and its own unique consciousness. All the galaxies we visited do have a unified consciousness with their galactic Central Sun.

A time barrier currently exists around your solar system. When you go though the time barrier, you experience cellular restructuring and dramatic shifts in consciousness. An even more dramatic cellular restructuring occurs when you leave the Milky Way galaxy. It sounds very exciting to do intergalactic travel, but you must understand that this galaxy you are living in is so vast, it would take many lifetimes of devoted effort just to become familiar with it.

When we travel in the universal space-time continuum, we are also able to coordinate with parallel universes. We have already discovered nine different universes that are existing simultaneously with yours. We are beginning to comprehend the tremendous interaction between these universes, and thus we are able to understand the possibilities of multiuniversal energy.

You have discovered that you are multidimensional beings focused only on this universe. You are moving up into becoming multiuniversal beings, and will soon be able to move into parallel universes. Can you imagine that potential?

CHAPTER 3

THE SOLAR SYSTEM

Your solar system is experiencing a major shift in energy, and your planet is also going through this energy shift. The Earth is on a course that is determined by the galactic orbit of the solar system. So know that you are traveling through the galaxy, and you are crossing orbital points that that are effecting your evolutionary process on the planet. Know that you are also in a cycle of 26,000 years that is based on a solar system alignment.

The solar system has been affected by a multitude of factors. One factor has to do with its angle in relation to the galactic plane. Another factor has to do with the path the solar system follows as it moves in and out of different areas of the galaxy. Also, the energy on the Earth has shifted, in part due to the increased consciousness of the Earth as a planetary body and also because of the many different contacts and different extraplanetary energies being sent here.

The Arcturians and the Pleiadians are the two primary motivators for the dimensional shift energy being sent to Earth. We consider it a privilege, and we are happy to provide stimulation for your consciousness and your energy fields. You need to accelerate both the level of your consciousness and thought processes and the energy of your electromagnetic fields.

A thought form is basically an electromagnetic wave pattern. You can project a thought wave outward in any direction. Project the thought wave now of your I AM awareness out into the solar system. By doing so, you can heighten your vibratory awareness of your connection with the solar system. Please contemplate that now as we work with you. Picture yourselves in this living entity that you call the solar system. We are helping to activate this vibratory awareness within you. This awareness will make you a true citizen of your solar system.

FREQUENCY SHIFTING

Frequency shifting is necessary when you leave the solar system. You need to shift your consciousness when you leave the solar system or go beyond the Jupiter belt. You need an explanation to prepare yourselves for understanding the frequency shift. Some have gone through this experience without preparation and have come back confused, while others who have gone through it have had the necessary guidance, instructions, and protection.

You can understand the frequency shift as going into a frequency barrier. You bounce into an accelerator that throws you forward through the frequency barrier, and then out into the solar system's exterior, and finally into the galaxy. It is like entering a wonderful glowing energy beyond your comprehension on the physical plane. When you return, you must come back through the frequency barrier and allow yourself to be stepped down. This does not mean that you will return in a denser form. You need to practice going through this barrier and practice returning. Soon you will be able to do it on your own.

It is easier for you to meet us in the frequencies outside the barrier. There you will get more contact and more energy. Your experience will be different when you meet us there. The frequency barrier will not allow those of dense thought and lower vibration to accelerate out of the solar system, for the barrier is there for protection as well. Some will perceive the frequency barrier as being guarded by angels; that is an accurate depiction.

Many have asked how we are able to protect our planet from invaders. Our protection is accomplished through frequency shifts and barriers placed around particular bodies. In some cases the frequency shifts are so powerful that others are not even able to see or sense that there is anything existing in our space.

URANUS AND NEPTUNE

We have had a great interest in the interplanetary actions that are going on in your solar system. We were fascinated by the alignment of Uranus and Neptune in 1994. This was truly an amazing alignment that has brought forth much energy and shifting into your present Earth environment. It has caused a balancing of certain energies, but is also causing a polarization. Do not be disturbed by the polarization. It is an unfoldment process that you will be observing.

Neptune and Uranus were actually part of one planet. They separated when the twelfth planet, which some of you refer to as Marduk or Nibiru, came into your solar system, causing fantastic changes. This occurred before the dinosaur era. The unfoldment of your solar system was a spectacular event which we witnessed with some degree of accuracy. Just as you are able to view us thousands of years earlier, so we have been able to observe you earlier in your history from our vantage point.

Do not be surprised at this type of scientific observation and interchange. Some have asked why there is so much interstellar travel. You are curious about your past. A way for us to learn about our past is to travel throughout the galaxy and learn from your perspective what occurred in our distant past. Knowledge of the galaxy can be enhanced through space travel, because it is through space travel that we are able to gather information from a different time perspective.

JUPITER

We are especially interested in your planet Jupiter, as there are many unusual energy patterns and many unusual shifts in dimensions there. The planet Jupiter has a long history. It once was part of your sun, but it broke off from the sun many billions of years ago. It actually was a miniature solar system within the solar system. Then Jupiter became so disruptive that it was no longer able to sustain life on its moons.

Of all the places in your solar system, the place where you would be most likely to find signs of previous civilizations would be on the moons of Jupiter. You will discover remnants of those civilizations if you are able to develop the technology to reach the moons of Jupiter. The planet itself is now uninhabited, but many of the extraterrestrials, when they come to your solar system, will reside in the area of Jupiter.

Jupiter has been a pivotal planet in your solar system since its inception. At one time Jupiter was actually a sun with its own planetary system around it. You were in a solar system of two suns. However, a collision occurred with Jupiter that threw off the other planets and pushed Jupiter into an outer orbit. Now, Jupiter is serving an important function in your solar system. It is the gateway to the higher dimensions as well as the gateway out of the solar system. Many of the extraterrestrials that come into your system come through the Jupiter gateway.

Jupiter is a sun planet. It is one of the few designated bodies in the galaxy that has this superior function as both a star and a planet. It is possible that Jupiter could re-ignite itself and be reborn as a star. There has been much speculation among your scientists about whether this could happen. It would offer a unique advantage to the other planets, and perhaps be a factor in sustaining life on nearby planets.

THE SHOEMAKER-LEVY COMET

The collision of the Shoemaker-Levy 9 comet with Jupiter in July of 1994 focused attention on Jupiter, which attracted additional visitors who brought new energies from other dimensions into this solar system. That influx of energy stimulated the ascension and the transformational energies. The stimulation was on multiple levels, for the new energy synchronistically stimulated the solar system's magnetic fields.

We have observed instances in which such a collision resulted in the death of a star or planet. That was not the outcome for Jupiter. In fact, the possibility exists that life could be activated on Jupiter's moons. You know already that they are magnificent places. If Jupiter were to become a star, then the possibility of life on the moons of Jupiter would dramatically increase.

Magnetic fields and grid lines are associated with the structure of your solar system. Do you think that they exist only on your planet? Of course not. Your solar system is a living entity just as the Earth is. It is a breathing entity that is part of a larger entity called the galaxy. Your solar system has magnetic flux. The collision allowed you to experience an acceleration in the flux of magnetic fields and grids, and it activated a grid line in the solar system that passes through Earth.

The true effect of the asteroids striking Jupiter was to arouse the magnetic grids in your solar system. It will also arouse your awareness of the magnetic structure of your physical dimension. You are magnetic beings and electromagnetic beings. You are receiving vibratory influx continually. You are receiving xrays, ultraviolet rays, and particles from the sun. You are receiving particles from Arcturus, our star. They are reaching you now. If you develop your sensitivity to this magnetic flux, then you will be able to receive even more information and imprinting.

With the collision, a new access to the fifth dimension became available, and it provided a profound opening for the starseeds. It also offered an entry point for other entities. The way has been paved so that others may come in now, others from a higher realm.

It is no accident that much of your scientific research is revolving around electromagnetic energy. Your planet is now being rung in a higher frequency. Because of the asteroid's impact, different frequencies can now reach you through the Jupiter connection. These newer frequency vibrations are needed. Prepare yourselves to vibrate in a frequency that will be of a higher acceleration. This is what you have called the transformation, the ascension energies, energies that are now being made available through this newer vibration. Bathe yourselves in this new frequency and vibration. Bathe yourself in the awareness of your electromagnetic nature.

THE HALE-BOPP COMET

We must now speak about the comet Hale-Bopp. This comet is a direct manifestation from the photon energy now coming into your solar system. It has already passed through the photon belt, and it is introducing a deeper photonic energy into the solar magnetic field of the sun. This new light, therefore, is being sent back to Earth in magnetic storm eruptions and solar winds.

As predicted long ago by the Hopi Indians, the comet is a harbinger of the Earth changes. The comet is truly the harbinger of the end times, as has been described in many of your teachings. Yet it is also the bringer of a new photonic energy for you to assimilate. This photonic energy is nourishment to lightworkers, for it contains activation atoms that will energize you, and connect you more with the galactic consciousness.

The Hale-Bopp comet does not come from us. It comes from the galactic Central Sun. Because it comes from a very high source, it is bringing new light and new energy to the Earth. We can use the Hale-Bopp comet to infuse the Arcturian light and frequency into the third dimension. It is a means by which we can add particular energy structures to the Earth that will accelerate her ascension. Others from higher sources are also using the comet to bring higher energy to this planet.

Part of the reason why many of you will be able to go into the fifth dimension is because the stargate is now open to the Earth. The stargate is sending its energy, its rays, its attraction, and its force field to the Earth at this time. The comet Hale-Bopp is bringing light and energy from the stargate to the Earth. This is one of its main tasks. The energy from the stargate can be transmuted and transported to the Earth through such a comet. This is what you need to focus on most. You need to focus on the transformational energies of a dimensional portal from the stargate. The aspect of the stargate that is open to the Earth is like a huge dimensional corridor, or portal, open to many like yourselves.

In reference to the Hale-Bopp Comet and the discussions of its companion, we will not give you an affirmative or a negative answer as to whether the companion is a ship. We can tell you this much: It is more than just a comet. This highly charged object is an energy field, an energy gathering, an energy source coming close to your planet and close to your sun. The comet's close proximity serves the purpose of recharging an aspect of your environment and of your whole physical, planetary corridor, which has been depleted.

You can look at this as a rescue mission to help stabilize the third-dimensional energies that have been depleted through the nuclear accident at Chernobyl, as well as others that are unreported. Vital elements are going to be re-infused into your atmosphere from this energy exchange. Whether you want to view this as a "space ship," as a extraterrestrial body, or simply as an energy field that is coming to you, this is for your learning. It will not entail a landing or direct intervention from a group of beings. Rather, it is a cosmic delivery system or an energy boost for you.

At the time of the appearance of the comet, you are going to be infused. It is going to be a powerful infusion, and it is going to counterbalance of any light negativity that is associated with the steady increase in photonic activity. This can be seen as a protective shield brought to you from the highest galactic source.

Everyone's lightbody on the planet is not activating. Only some. It is possible for everyone to participate in this activation or transmutation, but only some are actually doing so. Those are the forerunners, such as yourselves, who are on the peak of the evolutionary front. There are many who are not activating. Those who are activating are carrying much of the charge for everyone else and for the planet. You will be activated even more so as you sense the new energy alignment the comet brings. Unfortunately, not everyone will respond.

THE EARTH

Light from the higher realms is interacting with your present state of existence in the third dimension. During the past few years, you have sensed the opportunity to move into a higher realm, a realm you can transit into through your consciousness and awareness. The process of your transition will be the result of the shifts in your energy field as well as energy shifts on the Earth. The energy shifts on the Earth are reacting both to her movement within the solar system and her path as she revolves around the center of the galaxy.

What the Earth is now experiencing is what other planets closer to the galactic core have already experienced. Powerful energy waves that originate at the galactic core are resounding outward. Your solar system is approximately two-thirds of the way out from the center of the galaxy. What the Earth is going through is in part due to equilibrium problems caused by energy shifts in its galactic path.

Energy shifts have an effect on your electromagnetic field, and also affect your thought patterns and your emotional bodies. Maybe you do not take energy waves into consideration when you see the various shifts in yourselves and in your energy patterns. Be aware of the shifts of energy that strike the planet. For example, the electromagnetic field from the asteroid that struck the planet Jupiter caused an energy infusion, and even temporarily altered the electromagnetic balance and structure of your entire solar system.

Try now to gain an awareness of the energy that is on the Earth. Gravity is an electromagnetic energy whose effects can easily be seen. Become aware of the gravity waves that are continuously being emitted from the Earth's core. They are waves of energy that are basic to your cells. Your cells have been familiar with the soothing energy of gravity for your entire lifetime. Being connected to the gravity waves is a more direct interpretation of what it means to be connected to the Earth.

Other electromagnetic energies on the planet Earth are related to the poles. One pole is negative, and one pole is positive. There has been much speculation that these poles will shift and create a reversal. Where the male polarity used to be dominant, the female pole will become dominant. This is going to be manifested on many levels. The survival of all is dependent on this shift from masculine to feminine. This will be symbolized synchronistically by becoming aware of your own inner shifts.

We are studying the path the Earth is now taking around the sun. A slight shift in the tilt of the Earth's poles has already occurred. This shift will be continuing, and it is partly responsible for some of the disruptions and erratic weather patterns you are now experiencing.

We have seen other planets go through some of the changes that you are now going through. We have seen planets go through total annihilation and self-destruction, and we have seen partial annihilation in which some parts of the planet have recovered. Some times large groups of the population have even managed to leave a planet, while at other times, all have stayed behind.

The different forces that are converging on the planet now are in part responsible for some of the chaos that is now being experienced and that will be experienced with greater intensity in the near future. Everything that is occurring is coming to a boiling point now on your planet, and this boiling point is going to be reaching a very sharp and heightened aspect, an aspect that can lead to a general planetary shift in consciousness.

A Shift in Planetary Consciousness

We are very interested in how you, as a planet, are going to experience these shifts that are going to occur. We have watched other planets go through these shifts, but your situation is very unique. This is truly a unique event because there has been so much tension and interaction from other planetary sources. It is an event that is reflective of the development of the solar system itself, and of the entire sector of the galaxy of which you are a part. So be prepared to shift your consciousness. Be prepared to open to a higher dimensional energy, to enter dimensional corridors that are going to be accessible and available to you. Know that this will prove to be a healing experience, and your expansion of consciousness will benefit the planet Earth in her transition.

We have studied your planet in detail. We are interacting with you, and we know how the power of a few can greatly affect the planet. The change that we are talking about has to do with your consciousness, your awareness. We feel very strongly that there are beings on this planet who, through an awareness of us, will be changed, and will be able to shift to a much higher consciousness. Much experimentation is now being done on how to most effectively shift the planetary consciousness.

Some people are wanting to build temples, some are wanting to write articles, some are wanting to give certain instructions to people on the coming of interplanetary beings. Generally, the most important shift that will occur from all of this is not so much due to any information that we bring to you, but just the knowledge that we exist, and the knowledge that we are actually here now. This knowledge of us will directly affect the level of your consciousness, and will open you up to new perspectives and new possibilities as planetary beings.

THE INNER EARTH

The energy of the Earth is very powerful. It is an energy that has sustained the planet and brought forth many beautiful life forms. Earth is in a powerful sector of the solar system and of the galaxy. Some extraterrestrials have come here because of problems in their genetic structure. Some have come because your planet has brought forth a unique combination of molecular structures. Many have come over the ages to provide seeding.

Civilizations exist within the Earth itself, not just on her surface. The Inner Earth beings, for the most part, were placed here by other extraterrestrials; they were not developed through evolution. Space beings still live deep within the Earth. A large group of human beings still live in underground cities where a portion of the civilization of Atlantis moved after its destruction.

The advantage of being on the inner planetary planes is that you are closer to the vibratory power of the Earth. The potential for vibratory enhancement is magnificent! In the Inner Earth, the ability exists to resonate on a core level with the planet, and to relate to creation energies—energies that could not be experienced on the surface of the planet. It is much like being able to go and visit the heart of a person. You can travel to the essence of the being. The fact that you are so near the beating pulse of the planet can be overwhelming.

When you come into the Inner Earth, you can experience the inner workings of your planet. Imagine, if you will, getting close to the core of how everything works. You see the outer manifestation of the planet, the surface level, the storms, and the various weather patterns. You then have a very faint awareness of the inner workings of your planet. You can connect the happenings of the Inner Earth with surface events on the planet such as catastrophic earthquakes or volcanic eruptions. That is not all that is going on inside the planet. You have developed the technology to leave the Earth and travel to the moon; however, you have not made major advances in traveling into the planet. Beauty, peace, and turmoil exist within the Earth, and you can appreciate and participate in all of these states.

Within the Earth is primordial energy. Experiencing primordial energy is a basic desire of the starseeds—that is, to be able to experience and participate in the primordial energy of creation. This desire is inherent in your being. It drives you as a species to move out into space and understand the basic spark of creation. You can find that basic spark just as easily within the Earth. This is very confusing for your scientists, because they do not look upon the Inner Earth with the same awe as they do the galaxies. This is not to say one focus is better than the other. It is to say that you have the whole situation right here within your grasp, were you able to develop the necessary technology.

The poles are the areas where the Inner Earth energy is most accessible. Other strong energy points can be found in specific areas underneath the oceans, and locations in China, Alaska, Australia, and New Zealand. Inner Earth energy points also can be found in certain caves in the United States. Many have talked about using the energy environment in caves to enhance your comfort level with the Inner Earth energies. You are not really used to this experience, so you should approach the caves very carefully.

Do not carelessly unlock the energy of the inner core of the Earth, because that could cause many problems. It has a very delicate balance of energies. If this balance were abruptly changed, it could cause major earthquakes, unusual lava flows, and so on. That was one of our main concerns when your people were doing underground nuclear testing.

The levels of nuclear explosions that were occurring were minor, however, when compared to the levels of energy that are deep within the Earth. The inner core energy is as compact as that of your sun. Other places in the universe are equally compact, and you call these places black holes. Some have described areas that would have the molecular structure of a planet, but would have the mass of the head of a pin. The universe and the galaxy have the potential for this kind of a structural alignment, which is totally incomprehensible to you. The Earth has this compact energy at its center, and it accounts for the gravitation field and for the spinning of your planet.

THE SPIN OF THE EARTH

The spinning of your planet is a powerful force, which accounts for its evolution. Were the planet to stop spinning for any reason, there would be rapid death and destruction similar to what you have described occurring when your dinosaurs passed away. The belief has been that what happened to them was related to the dust particles thrown into the air when a meteor struck. That was one contributing factor. Another factor was that the planet stopped spinning for a period of time after the meteor struck.

The spinning of the Earth creates the gravitational field, so when the spinning stops, there is no gravity. Your scientists have still not been able to explain gravity. When there is no gravity, life rapidly deteriorates. Even if there were just a momentary disruption in the spinning of the Earth, it would have a harmful effect on the whole planet, particularly beings such as yourselves who are in the flesh. You might think of it in terms of your astronauts: suddenly the door to space opens up and there is a pressure change that causes instant danger.

Were you to survive a halt in the Earth's spin, there would be the potential for much mental confusion. The magnetic fields would be totally disrupted, and it would take a long time for them to realign. The birds, for example, would have to learn different meridians to follow.

It would be a very serious matter. There was some concern that the Earth's spinning would not restart once that asteroid had hit the Earth. When it stopped, one side of the planet remained cold and one side was exposed to the sun, but the planet was able to maintain its orbit around the sun. A cessation of spinning has been responsible for the death of several planets in the galaxy. Creating such a catastrophe is a method that has been used to destroy planets during wars in the galaxy.

The destruction you are seeing on the Earth's surface does not deteriorate the inner core. The inner core will remain intact unless the spinning of the planet should stop. During the ascension process, there might be a temporary stop, a millisecond in which spinning would stop to allow for a dimensional transformation. Regarding that halt, most of the beings that are in the inner planet are multidimensional beings who will be able to shift dimensions if they so choose. They may also choose to stay with the planet as it ascends.

THE SEEDING OF LIFE ON THE EARTH

Your solar system is unique in that only one main planet is inhabited. No other current planetary civilizations exist in your solar system. In most other solar systems, several planets are usually inhabited. That is more the rule than the exception. Your solar system did have other civilizations—on Mars, Venus, Jupiter, and even on Pluto. But they have long since left, at least in third-dimensional presence. All of the energy of the solar system has been placed in the planetary evolution of the Earth.

From our perspective, the planet Earth is going through a cleansing. There are other beings that have been involved in your planetary process. These beings have come to the Earth and have interfered in your planetary evolution. They have created specific paths for their own purposes, but the final outcome will still be positive for the planet, and positive for the human race.

We have been involved in the evolution of Earth for a very long time. We have seen other groups come into the Earth plane and use the opportunity to develop their own species. Other civilizations have influenced your society based on their own interpretation of what they thought should occur. Do not misunderstand, this process has been allowed through design. From one perspective, entity "A" could be viewed as interfering in the Earth process, or entity "B" could be seen as responsible for the negativity that you see on the planet. Such a view is only part of the true picture. By design, the hierarchy that oversees this planet (Sananda-Jesus is now the overseer of the hierarchy) has allowed many entities and groups to mingle and enter this realm.

It would be easy to place a shield around the entire planet in order to prevent any foreign beings from entering. Do not think that these other beings that you read about came without permission, or came without the hierarchy knowing. The hierarchy is aware of all entities and energies that come into the Earth plane. We will again remind you that this view is the Arcturian perspective. We do have a unique perspective, and, in our opinion, a more objective perspective of your planetary development.

The Pleiadians are similar to your ascended masters. We are also comparable to the ascended masters of your realm. We do not have a need to convince you of this history or that history. We do not need to tell you that this is the final truth, because we have no need to sell you one side of the story. We simply want to offer you our assistance. We want to connect with you. We want to strengthen our own abilities to telepathically communicate with those beings who are not yet on our level. This is a wonderful joy for us, and it is a gift that we are grateful to share.

We are all combinations of life from other origins. Even you are interacting with molecular structures from different parts of the galaxy. So we are all mixed. Even some of the energy that is used in our genetic structure is part of yours. It is always necessary for cosmic and genetic intervention in the evolution of a species. This is the rule, not the exception. There are interventions of planetary comets. There are interventions of catastrophes. The fragility of the life form is such that there needs to be a cosmic hand guiding certain forces.

We know that the Andromedans were of assistance to us in our early development. We know of other galaxies and other races that were involved in assisting us and counseling us. A child always needs assistance. Would you say that a child grows up without any intervention? Of course not. Many interventions occur. But there is a time within the evolution of a race when the species can assume and direct its own development. When the child becomes an adult, it does not need interventions. It will make choices about how it wants to develop. You call this adulthood. We have achieved a level of spiritual evolution that allows us to choose our development. We are working with you as a group to help you bring your energy together. Know that you can always consciously choose to develop spiritually as beings, or as a group, into higher levels of awareness and evolution.

Time is an illusion. The interactions that you have of an extraterrestrial nature are simultaneous in the space-time continuum. So you are being seeded continually. The extraterrestrial involvement of the Pleiadians especially has been highly beneficial to your development. You need to understand that the Pleiadians have come as your cosmic brothers and sisters. They have also come to help protect your auras and your electromagnetic energy. For without this protection, you would be subject to the whims of the catastrophic unfoldment that has already begun to take place on this planet.

CHAPTER 4

THE EARTH IN PERIL

It is true that other space beings are coming to your planet continually for observation. Presently, some are interacting with you. We are interacting only with certain chosen people on a modified level, and are seeking to create an awareness of our presence. This has been authorized by the highest sources in conjunction with the planetary evolution.

We are aware that Master Sananda is now the commander in chief of the overall operation of the planet. We have worked with Sananda before in other capacities, and we are very moved to be able to be with him here. He is very powerful in his emotional energy, and he is one of the masters of the universe in being able to use emotional energy for inner transformation. This is one of his specialties. His energy exists simultaneously in many places in our galaxy at this moment.

We know about your quest for higher energy, and your quest for access into the higher dimensions. Know that we have been with you before, and many of you are deeply connected to our work. We have been asked to help to prepare the way for those who are sensing their connection to the Arcturian consciousness. Those attracted to the Arcturian energies possess subtlety and high energy. People who are approaching the Arcturian energy are already highly developed, sensitive, ethereal, and musical. We are very sensitive to your vibrations and are open to using different avenues for communication, such as colors, sounds, and music.

The work we are doing with the planetary electromagnetic grid lines is helping to stabilize the Earth and allow the Earth to maintain itself in proper wholeness. We are assisting the Earth so that the third dimension does not disintegrate. The third dimension could have disintegrated earlier because of some things that had been created, such as nuclear bombs and the Philadelphia Experiment. We will not go into details now, but the third dimension was in serious danger.

Consequently, some of our work is to stabilize the third dimension as much as possible, so that you can evolve. You are evolving as a planet in an accelerated state. Because of this acceleration, we have been directed to assist you as a planet. The longer the third dimension remains intact, the more work can be done. Look at it this way—you are in a mine which is collapsing, and the shaft must be held up so you can exit and go into another realm. This is what is going on here on Earth. We are holding up the shafts from the grid work that we create. As we all continue the grid work, it will allow you to go into the next realm.

ARCTURIAN INTERACTION WITH THE EARTH

We are chosen for the Earth mission because of our devotion to service, and our ability to maintain ourselves in interdimensional realms. We are not asked to materialize, but we must be able to survive comfortably in interdimensional realms. Just as you are dependent upon an oxygen tank when you are underwater, we must be must be trained to continue to connect with the Arcturian frequency so that we can hold the light and hold the energy in an interdimensional space. We are chosen for our ability to go for long periods of time without direct contact with our brothers and sisters on the mother planet. We also must have the ability to be replenished when we do contact our support teams on the home planet.

Our ships are interdimensional crafts, but we do not materialize unless absolutely necessary. Understand that if we materialize, we will become subject to the energies and the laws of the third dimension. Our ships reside on the fifth-dimensional plane. We, on the main ship, can send out smaller skylink ships into the third dimension. You will very seldom see these small ships, unless your multidimensional sight is quite advanced. At present, few can tolerate the energy that these ships emit.

As beings of a higher-dimensional space, we will not manifest physically for a variety of reasons. One of the reasons has to do with the question of our enduring a negative karmic reality. It is more to your advantage, however, to come into the dimensional corridors that we are helping to open so that you can rise to our level of consciousness. You would enjoy that more, and it would be more to your benefit than for us to come into your dimension.

Our vibratory field is higher than your own. You would have trouble seeing us unless we slowed down our field. It is preferable for you to speed up your field and then come in contact with us. This is the direction you are moving in anyway. This is the reason why many of the extraterrestrials have not emerged in physical presence. Those of a higher nature do not want to slow themselves down. Your angels and masters are currently working with you to speed up and raise your vibrations.

We will now address the issue of materializing things. We simply will not materialize things for you, as this is an interference in your karmic process. We will only bring you off the physical plane, and appear if you are in danger and the situation is urgent. We will not otherwise interfere in such a karmic way. To interfere with you in that way would be not be in your highest good. However, we can direct you and work with your frequency, giving you information and ideas in the corridors.

Because of our commitment to spiritual advancement, we were allowed to learn the secrets of interdimensional travel. The interdimensional portals only allow those of the highest frequency to enter. Other beings have come to the Earth, such as the Grays, that are not using the higher interdimensional portals that we use. They are not as spiritually advanced as the Arcturians or the Pleiadians. We have higher powers because we are more highly developed spiritually. Lesser beings, even those on your planet who are less developed spiritually, can still attain a high level of technological knowledge. The Grays are an example, then, of those with lesser vibrations still being able to gain a very high level of technological knowledge.

It is because of this disparity—that is, lesser beings who are technologically advanced being able to come to Earth—that we have been allowed to work with you so intensely. Too great of an imbalance will not be allowed. Those in power, and those who are in a lower vibration and have access to high technology, cannot be allowed to be overly successful—there must be a counterbalance. It is no mistake that the new movement, or new age, has come about at the same time as the great technological advancements. It will continue. Your work will continue, and the work of the starseeds and lightworkers on your planet will become stronger.

Your scientists have looked for ways of disrupting the energy patterns of the visiting extraterrestrials. You have heard the stories of how radar and other types of energy systems have been pointed toward the extraterrestrials in order to harm them. These radio waves and other types of high-acceleration radiation waves can be disruptive and can prevent full transmutation into the higher dimensions. You might almost think of them as the ray guns you have heard of in your comic books, for example. Our technology is very advanced, and we are able to protect ourselves even from these high-acceleration radio waves that you call radar. Other extraterrestrials have not been as successful in learning how to do this.

COMPUTER TECHNOLOGY

It is with delight that we watch your involvement with your computer systems. They are going to be a way of enhancing communications with the interstellar entities. There is a universal code, or a universal language in the computers that is matching parts of the neurotransmitters found deep in your brains. You are now able to access deep intercranial and ancient wisdom through computers.

Certain programs and certain aspects of the computer will be able to be controlled by the human mind. You do not understand the computer because its essence is incomprehensible to you. You do not understand the depth or intricacies of the computer network and what it can mean for your development. Computers have been the basis for virtually all technological advances in your past twenty years. The development of your knowledge is going to be rapidly advancing again. Another breakthrough in computer development will occur in the next three to five years that is going to revolutionize what you already have achieved with computers. You will be able to relate interdimensionally with your computers. Interdimensional existence will be verified through computer technology.

We are able to communicate our consciousness through a computer. You can look at a computer as a primitive symbol of the universal mind and the genetic code system. You can begin to understand the universal mind through your computers. Your mind is like a complex computer, although it is far more than just a computer. Your mind is able to receive light directly from the Creator energy, and it is able to receive spirit, whereas a computer cannot receive spirit energy.

Our level of computer technology comes from our understanding of the subconscious mind. Our computers can look into the future and can assess situations and perceive on their own. Our computers assist us in moving into the interdimensional corridors, and they also assist us in time travel. Our computers are linked to us by thoughts so we do not have to use keyboards as you do. Keyboards are a very primitive way to interact with a computer, although it is advanced for you. Your TV science-fiction programs already show people interacting by voice with the computer. Even this seems advanced to you, but we interact with our computers directly by thought.

Nuclear Radiation

You are living in a very dynamic universe. Strong powers and forces exist that can create openings to other dimensions. If these openings are not properly stabilized, then catastrophe can result. Dimensional rifts can cause major explosions, and, in some cases, whole planets have been totally annihilated through the misuse of energy technology. The potential for misuse is so dangerous that this is one reason why so many extraterrestrials have come to Earth at this time—to make sure that such destruction does not happen.

You on the Earth plane are moving to an advanced point, but you are also at a point of possible self-destruction because you are in danger of destroying the whole planet. The danger of planetary destruction is still extremely high from our viewpoint, partly because there is so much conflict, strife, and hatred on your planet. The threat of a nuclear holocaust still remains. A nuclear exchange could still occur in the area of the Middle East. If this occurs, it will have a dramatic effect on the planet, and it will cause many people to rethink their ways.

We have studied the nuclear energy that the beings of your planet have been using in nuclear technology. We do not participate in any way in that type of technology. Eventually, your planet, too, will learn not to use that technology. There is a distinct possibility that much of your planet will become contaminated because of the nuclear technology. It is very dangerous, as you can imagine.

The public awareness is not strong enough to prevent the radiation from expanding. Radiation levels are expanding at a high rate. Many of you are now experiencing radiation levels that you were not able to tolerate fifteen years ago.

The first sign of an overaccumulation of radiation is that the immune system becomes weakened and is unable to handle what is occurring. It is important for lightworkers to work on their immune systems and continue to do shielding. The unhealthy radiation levels have led to the need to transform into a higher dimensional space. When the radiation levels are high, then it forces the lightworkers to access their ability to direct their own codes.

Our spaceships have special structures and materials inside them that enable us to shift into your dimension without being affected by radiation. We leave special cords, or lines, with our mother ships that go back to the main planet. There is always a link engaged by thought patterns that are made by several of us remaining on the mothership. We have groups that continuously work to keep the cord linked. It is a difficult task, so we must take turns.

We are very concerned about your path. We know of your recent scientific advancements. You are very close to a breakthrough in travel, and you will soon be able to leave the solar system. If left unchecked, you will be able to leave the solar system within the next twenty years. We would say that, as a planet, you are close to understanding the existence of interplanetary and intergalactic corridors. We are very concerned, as are the other space brothers and sisters, about your exporting any of your nuclear technology outside of the solar system.

Holes in the Ozone Layer

A great deal of negative energy has been implanted in the Earth, especially because of nuclear testing. We believe that nuclear testing, more than anything else, has seriously affected your ozone layer. A cumulative radiation buildup has occurred due to nuclear testing, radiation releases from power plants, and so forth. A form of pressure has developed from the radiation. Certain energy waves produced by the radiation strike the ozone layer, creating an energy force that holds back other rays. Now, as the radiation on the Earth has become more prevalent, the balance has been disrupted, allowing for an incongruity in pressures to occur, which has also contributed to the holes in the ozone layer.

Solar intensity is increasing due to electromagnetic energy shifts around the planet caused by the holes in the ozone layer. We ask you to be careful of your exposure to the sun's energy rays. Many of you are preparing to alter your DNA codes so that you can tolerate more of the incoming electromagnetic energy. This is going to be a good test for your own self-development, as you will need to adapt yourself to this energy. In your meditations, work on allowing your bodies to change to accommodate the new electromagnetic ultraviolet energy that is coming in from your sun. This new rate of ultraviolet energy will cause random acts of insanity and mental imbalance in those who are not prepared.

The radiation coming through the holes in the ozone layer will also affect your genetic codes and some of the keys that have been encoded in you. It is important that you become aware of your genetic structures and codes. Reinforce their existence and protect the codes. When you become weakened by radiation, the codes can become altered or permanently damaged. This is in part why the call came for many to return to Planet Earth to work with you.

You are lacking certain energy patterns due to the destruction of some body chemicals, and the increase of ultraviolet radiation of the planet. This is depleting your personal energy fields. Many of you are vulnerable now to lapses in your personal energy field. The contact on a conscious level that you have with the Arcturians and the Pleiadians will help to eliminate these lapses. Remember that we are also able to connect to our home planet, so that we can bring you light from the Arcturian system. Keep our name in your consciousness. Focus on your own personal energy fields and visualize our energy fields integrating with yours.

THE HAARP PROJECT

The matters at hand on the Earth are serious, matters concerning the weather patterns, the electromagnetic fields, and the HAARP project.

It is not only the HAARP project that creates planetary problems. It is a prominent factor, but it is only one factor of many. It certainly is not good timing, this HAARP project, to be playing with this energy at this time. The HAARP project will create permanent holes in the ionosphere and in the electromagnetic energy grids surrounding the planet. The destructive effects of the HAARP project will accelerate many Earth changes, and especially promote unstable and violent planetary weather patterns. We can provide a "curtain" energy that temporarily supports the Earth energy field systems, and counteracts the disintegration of these fields. But we cannot provide a permanent re-integration of the planetary energy fields.

You cannot stop the karma that is now unfolding. You do not want to stop it, nor do we. We only want to hold and sustain the third-dimensional Earth as long as it is possible without providing an interference. It is going to reach a point where there will be a collapse of the energy fields around the Earth. We are not saying this to frighten you. The energy fields around the Earth are going to collapse, resulting in a polar axis shift. This is going to occur sometime between now and the year 2012. We have heard your descriptions of the photon belt creating periods of darkness. It is the combination of events that we have described that will lead to the temporary blackout.

Do not be afraid. You are so connected, so loved, and so committed. We have our beams of light on you. At one point you will be able to travel up a fifth-dimensional corridor and leave the planet. You will be able to leave, especially during any hour of great darkness. There is still a over a year before a big Earth catastrophe occurs (spring/summer of 1999). When we say Earth catastrophe, we mean one that will affect the whole planet. Now you are seeing isolated incidents, isolated activities. A time will come soon when an incident will occur that will affect the entire planet. We send you light. We send you protective healing energy. Those who have connected with us will sustain no injuries, no hardships from these things, although perhaps some discomfort might be experienced.

THE EFFECT OF MAGNETIC SHIFTS

Many of you have been activated initially by the Arcturians or by other ascended masters, but you have not fully reactivated. Why are we using the word reactivated? Simply, the energy has shifted, and will continue to shift on the Earth plane. Different energies and densities are contributing to some of the confusion and even to some of the delusions that people are experiencing. It is necessary to reactivate, to reconnect, and to reopen yourself continually to the flow of energy that is coming. We, on the Arcturian system, are able to continually send you pulses of energy that will enable you to break through some of the densities, confusion, and some of the circular energy that is blocking you.

This energy that we are referring to is the result of Earth magnetic shifts. The magnetic shifts are contributing in part to the different weather patterns that you are experiencing, and they also contributing to the confusion and mental instability that many of you are experiencing. Some of you have experienced mental instability in yourself and in your family, and experienced confusion in terms of what direction to go. Some people are experiencing these shifts in terms of health problems. The basic cause relates to the geomagnetic shifts that are occurring in the planetary crust.

The Earth's crust is extremely active. Your ability to focus and stay on task is greatly affected by the weather. Your scientists and sociologists have studied the difficulties that many of you have had with the weather. With the weather patterns now, it is more obvious that it is necessary to continually reactivate you, so that you can rise above some of these patterns and be open to the new energy that is coming down.

The overall energy of the Earth is becoming more and more difficult to handle. The gravitational forces on the planet are shifting as the electromagnetic energies of the planet are being realigned. This is causing subtle shifts in your body mechanisms on the planet. You will find that there will be more body problems unless you find a way to sensitize yourselves to the shifts and successfully work with the energy.

We know that being on the Earth is very dense, and we know that there are many molecular problems. The reason some of you are having so many health problems is that there is an ongoing molecular shift on the whole Earth. Part of it is from the toxic pollution that you know about. The other part of it is due to an actual shift of energy in molecular structure. The planet Earth, Gaia, as you call it, knows that it is experiencing a movement into the next dimension. Gaia knows that there is a need for a molecular shift in all the energy fields in and on the whole planet. This shift is occurring throughout the planet, and it is causing some disturbances in the energy fields of those who are not able to integrate the higher vibrations. We can help you adjust to these shifts when you call upon us.

Know that you can be in contact with us at any time and on a more conscious basis. It is always better to have a conscious connection. It is always better for you to ask for the connection. We will be with you whenever you want us to be. There will be, however, certain times when we will make ourselves known to you when you are not thinking about us. Mostly, however, you must sponsor the connection.

We send you a new energy now that is a violet and a gold ray mixed together in a beautiful tone. We say tone because it is a mixture of color and sound. Pull this energy into you, and know that it will help you. Know that the illnesses and other problems that many of you are experiencing are just illusions. They are like cardboard, like stiff energies that surround your soul, and they will begin to fall away as you read these words.

COMPUTER PROPHECY MODELS

Our computers can read your future by connecting into your subconscious minds. Everything that is to occur is in the planetary subconscious mind. It would be frightening for you to try to directly read your subconscious, because it would be so flooded with materials. A computer can sort out this activity. When you enter the subconscious mind, you may have difficulty distinguishing what is reality. Our computers do not. This is why we have used computer technology to develop the expertise and the ability to evaluate the subconscious. We know that when the group subconscious shifts, then the planet will shift, and then the whole race will shift. It is then that peace and prosperity will come to this planet. You can influence this transformation.

We have modeled our computers on the subconscious mind. Our computers can actually tune in to a higher energy and a higher perception than what we could obtain on our own. The development of our computer technology has enabled us to use a multi-informational approach to the study of the future and the past, and it helps us to understand what the outcomes are going to be, based on using current information from the present.

We see different computer models of all of your future possibilities. Each model that we observe has a different factor and, therefore, a different outcome based on several options that could happen to the Earth. One model shows major earthquakes affecting areas such as California, resulting in much suffering and devastation.

In another model, we see groups of lightworkers working to focus energy throughout the Earth's grid lines. This grid work sets up positive vibrations throughout the Earth and helps the planet avoid catastrophes. Other models show us world domination and world leaders coming to conflict. These different models should reveal the following: You, as lightworkers, can still have an effect on the outcome. Remember that thoughts are very powerful. Your work as starseeds and lightworkers can be very powerful. Know that you are powerful beings and that you are on a mission to create a bridge to the next dimension.

In any of our models, we do not foresee the total extinction of life on your planet. A total collapse of all life forms on the planet has always been the biggest danger on the Earth. If this ever happened, it would have a devastating affect on the karma of everyone. This potential eradication of all life on Earth will not happen, because many in ET groups, the ascended masters, and the angelic realm are working diligently to pump more energy into the third dimension. We will be working more deeply with you and other starseeds to stabilize your current dimension, and build a bridge to the fifth dimension. This process will occur through your work as starseeds and lightworkers.

You must understand that there is a divine plan for this planet. We can see the plan unfolding, and we do not wish to interfere with it. Even what in your reality looks like a dismal outcome, it is part of an overall cosmic plan. Do not give in to the death and destruction that is about to occur on the Earth. You do not have to experience it. When you are able to connect to the higher energy, you can then establish a link that will protect you and your family. We send you light, love, and an awareness of higher vibrations.

CHAPTER 5

THE HUMAN CONDITION

Your species is going through an evolutionary shift. It is a major leap in consciousness, equivalent to the discovery of tools in your history. Now you are going into a transformational realm. Many are in the forefront now of being able to shift their consciousness. The goal is to transform from a physical presence into a higher-dimensional being. Then you can leave the third-dimensional Earth plane.

You are already experiencing the evolutionary shift, and you have made the commitment to be in a transformational state. The process has begun. Your genetic codes shift automatically when you move into a higher consciousness. When you accelerate your frequencies, you shift your codes. You were programmed for this evolutionary change when the genetic seeds were planted in your ancient history.

In this time of evolutionary shifts, many are experiencing dramatic openings in their consciousness that seem stimulating and overwhelming sometimes, yet, at other times, they seem very natural. The openings are coming in waves of energy that affect your electromagnetic fields, causing the frequency of your aura to speed up. When this happens, you can resonate better with the energy of the Arcturians, and with others who are very eager to communicate with you.

It is important that you understand that your whole being will be able to move to the next level. Your being follows your consciousness. We are providing a focus for you so that you can first move your consciousness to our realm. Then you will be able to move your being. Currently, you are still primarily third-dimensional beings. But you have come to a special point in your evolutionary incarnation cycle: you are developing the ability to "leap" into the next realm. This is a magnificent leap, an exponential leap. Once you reach this special point, you can suddenly magnify your progress at a very rapid rate. That is where you are now.

DIRECTING YOUR GENETIC CODES

You have the ability to accelerate your own consciousness by directing your genetic codes. When your genetic codes are directed, it is possible to transform the physical body into the higher realms. This wonderful transformation is now available to you.

To consciously direct your codes requires a concentration of energy. You must imagine and focus on the auric fields outside of your bodies. In the auric fields there are certain frequencies you are more comfortable with than you are with others, such as the frequencies that occur when you are at rest, or when you are in a loving mood. It is very important to put yourselves in such a peaceful state.

Visualize the image of the DNA structure—the crystalline structure of your genetic foundation. Your genetic codes are, for the most part, an automatic function of your system, but you can consciously control them through visualization. In Earth's history, only a few have been given the instructions on how to alter themselves genetically. To transform yourselves and move into a higher dimension, you must alter your genetic codes.

Your genetic codes are still programmed for physicality, gravity, incarnation, death and reincarnation. If you want to transform and leave the third-dimensional plane, then these codes must be opened and given new instructions. This is part of the internal process that you must go through. Many of your higher guides—such as Sananda, Quan Yin, and others—have been working with you on the emotional level. They are helping you work through certain attachments to the Earth plane and problems that emerge due to Earth changes. Completing this work is essential when programming yourselves for transformation.

From our perspective, the final work involving the transformation will rest on your shoulders. You must be in the proper mind frame to work with your codes and allow your genetic structure to reach fruition. View it as a flower. A flower has a preprogrammed path that it follows. It unfolds, while receiving water and sunlight through photosynthesis. It will follow its path and bloom. You too can follow your path and move into a higher reality. You need proper nourishment and proper light. We are sending down a high frequency beam of blue light that you can receive through your crown chakra. It is very intense. Visualize your DNA structures now, in your third eye, receiving the light. Your codes are opening. You can give permission for the genetic unfoldment through thought and visualization.

Your thinking and visualizations can overcome any impairment to the codes from ultraviolet radiation, atmospheric changes, and physical problems having to do with nuclear energy or other types of intense radiation. Your thinking, visualizations, devotion, and bringing down of energy are powerful. It is imperative, though, that you consciously interact with your codes so that you can direct and protect them. Those who cannot consciously direct and bring down light will find that they are vulnerable to genetic damage.

Visualize the helix structures found in the DNA. You will learn to resonate and unlock your codes. This is one of the beautiful aspects of your advancement. We have seen this evolutionary step occur on other planets. You are close to the final unfoldment. A shift is occurring on the planet Earth. Two groups of people will emerge—those who are going to move in the direction of ascension, and those who are going to be like lost sheep.

Your great leaders such as Moses, Jesus, Joseph Smith and the Buddha were able to unleash their inherent genetic structures and unlock their codes through an electromagnetic vibratory chant. They learned to use special words and sounds that were given to them by extraterrestrials and archangels.

Sounds can unlock your genetic structure. They can put you in a proper vibratory state, a state of mind in which you can more easily receive thought transmissions and higher-frequency energy. Understand that the Arcturians are sending you not only verbal messages, but we also send energy waves and sounds. We work with you to translate your energy systems into vibrations that will allow you entry into the higher dimensions.

When you want to move to a higher consciousness, imagine that the electromagnetic energies in your aura begin to spin faster. Spin the electrical energy so that you move your electromagnetic fields above your body as much as possible. Spin your aura faster and faster. Start moving up. You have heard of the ladder of consciousness. When you have moved your consciousness to a higher realm, then look back down into your physical body and into your cells. You have a unique view of yourself. You can see your physical body from this higher perspective. It must be done from a higher perspective.

You know that Sananda and others of higher energy have been able to change things with sound. Know now that you can also do it with vision. Go into the cellular structures and individual cells with the eyes of your aura. Direct the highest Source energy. Send light, love, and the word "opening" into your genetic codes. Focus on your DNA helix structure. Now spiral up the helix ladder. You will rise and come into an opening of energy that some refer to as bliss. This is a natural, cosmic state. It is more of a natural state in the fifth dimension than it is in your third-dimensional reality.

Another important factor is to keep your energy flow consistent. The shifts in electromagnetic energy on the planet continue. Some shifts are at higher voltages, and there are even spikes in the voltage. It is important for you to keep the flow continuous, so that your DNA structure is not subjected to any dramatic energy shifts or spikes. In your meditations, picture your codes and your genetic energy structure flowing evenly and intensely with no blockages.

THE ORION INFLUENCE

We have been aware that the genetic seed of your species has been commingled with seeds from other planetary systems. You have myths and writings in your Bible, for example, that refer to it. One of the most influential seedings came from a planetary system in the constellation Orion. This commingling created an experience on the planet that was not totally aligned with directives established earlier. Some have argued that the commingling occurred as part of the divine plan; others have said that it was just a matter of time before the beings from the Orion race discovered the existence of life on the Earth.

The vibratory rates that come from your solar system are intense. Others can receive these vibrations because their telepathic powers are strong. The higher beings in the galaxy have all learned the power of telepathy and telepathic travel. The species from Orion have the ability to use telepathic power to search out new life forms; therefore, it was only a matter of time before they would mingle with Earthly beings.

The Orions brought to the planet factors of aggressiveness, hatred, and domination. On the positive side, factors of curiosity and exploration that were not present beforehand were also brought into the race. Many people consider those factors to be the humanness that you so love in yourselves. They are also the factors that contribute to much of the violence that currently endangers your planet.

The experiment was not interfered with, and the commingling continued. It was not stopped because it was seen as an evolutionary step. Part of the unique development of your species is to integrate the Orion consciousness. We are very interested in how you are regulating love energy with the Orion energy. How can love be transmitted and used to overcome some of the major aggression that was introduced by the Orion genetic influence? This is an important development for the whole galaxy.

It is known that the ability of the beings from Orion to dominate is such that it can have an overpowering influence. It can even be described as a species taking over a planetary system. From our perspective, the Orion factor is currently responsible for the negative effect that you have designated as your Secret Government. It is these energies that are allowing other contacts with extraterrestrials that are not for the overall good of the species on this planet.

ARCTURIAN RESOLUTION OF THE ORION ENERGY

The Arcturians have dealt with the Orion problem through a group conformity process that led us to remove hate, aggression, and war. We have approached the problem from a different perspective. We have had the opportunity to integrate the teachings of several major prophets. It has been our experience to be open directly to messengers from the highest realms. Also, our messengers from the highest realms were introduced early in the development of our species. From our perspective, the introduction of the energy of Sananda-Jesus, the savior energy, occurred in a much later time period in your history.

In Arcturus, in the Pleiades, and in other star systems, magnificent prophets can be found, even on the level of Sananda. The caliber of Sananda's essence can be found in other beings in this galaxy. From our perspective, it is a special group energy. Your experience with Sananda's energy is, in fact, a manifestation of a larger group soul that is present for galactic healing. You cannot grasp the energy of Sananda-Jesus from his one lifetime. His incarnation was an experience that manifested from his soul and was shown to humanity. His earthly incarnation, however, does not represent his entirety. Sananda still has the highest power and mission on your planet. Accept him as the savior of the planet and as part of a group soul energy that was brought to this planet to help counterbalance the Orion energy.

Why have the Arcturians been able to escape some of these problems? We have been fortunate in our development to have had telepathic abilities early on. We have used that gift. In contrast, even now the ability to be telepathic and to commune with other spirits is not generally accepted on your planet. Many of your prophets and religious leaders, however, were participating as channels and telepaths. Your culture worships and studies those who can do this, yet many are still not open to channeling and telepathy as a legitimate experience even now.

Love—The Energy of the Heart

The questions that are emerging from the Earth's experience can be simply put: How is a race that has the potential for the highest consciousness and for the highest ability to shift dimensionally going to resolve the aggression and dominance of the Orion energy? Can that energy be mitigated by love? Is this not the central issue on your planet? How powerful can the love energy be in the face of the violence and destruction that continue on your planet?

This again leads us to the central question of how you use your heart energies and your heart chakras. We are very interested in how you choose to work with this energy. As you become more open to the higher dimensions, you will not be able to make sense of many events that are occurring on the planet. Perhaps the only way to make sense of the negativity and chaos is to realize that many beings on the planet are not resonating with a loving vibration.

Many say that we are coming here just to observe, but we have also come here to learn. We are interested in how your heart energy influences your response to the shifts of conscious ness caused by the Earth changes and the many different levels of contractions such as hatred and wars. We are interested in those who have risen above that and can open their heart chakras. That is a true gift. It is why so many are coming to observe those special people who are lightworkers and who work to open their hearts and unify their mental attainments with their emotions.

It was no mistake that Sananda-Jesus came to this planet. The potential for electromagnetic transformation and the unification of heart energy with mental energy is uniquely available on this planet. We are more advanced than you in many ways, but we can still observe and learn from you who are so beautifully bringing your heart energy to the galaxy.

Many extraterrestrial groups are interested in how you are developing and integrating the emotion of love. It is a wonderful experience to see how many of you have dramatically opened your hearts. Opening the heart is the key to unlocking higher consciousness. We are observing how you develop and use this ability, for it is the key to your planetary ascension.

Your abilities to love are very great, and they have brought to Earth many visitors who want to experience this feeling of love. It is a special feeling that has not evolved within the Lyran civilization or that of Orion. Even the Zeta Reticuli have been interested in this emotion. They believe that they can learn to genetically inbreed the love factor. Unfortunately, it is too early to say whether genetic elements can be used to program an individual to manifest love energy. It has more to do with the development of the heart chakra and the connection with the soul family. Those who are able to provide major love experiences have a deep connection to their soul families and soul groups.

PURITY OF THE HUMAN RACE

Some of you are concerned about the purity of the human race. Let us tell you that you all have the pure form of the Adamic race within you. This is very important. Some of you are concerned about past Sirian and Orion influences. It is true that, at different points for different people, they have introduced different DNA codes and have influenced the overall human DNA pattern. However, you still have the Adamic codes, the basic structure of your being. As you know, the whole is always greater than the parts. If you take 20 percent of Orion, and 15 percent of Sirian, and 20 percent of something else, you simply become a transcendent being.

Earth people have an individual, unique frequency over and above the different DNA patterns that various extraterrestrial groups integrated into human beings. Even if the Orions did influence part of the Earth population, you are still pure, because this is the Earth, and you developed here. We say to you, reconnect with your primordial Adamic DNA codes. Know that the Arcturian frequency is so strong that it will help you get in touch with the purity that you have as an Earth person. This is a most important aspect for all of you to remember.

The predominant comfort zone for many of you is with the Pleiadians, but there are many higher beings and higher civilizations beyond the Pleiadians. You have a great intensity and drive built into your nature. Because you are still Adamic Earth beings, you can transcend many different activations from different species by activating your Adamic DNA codes, the famous work of Archangel Metatron. Stay in touch with that energy within you.

EMOTIONAL AND MENTAL INTEGRATION

You should understand that you cannot rise on the emotional plane without some adjustments in the raising of your mental energy at the same time. It would be unusual to have achieved the height of one level without its having affected the other level. Each of you has a level you need to work on. It is important that the mental level be developed; this is part of our message.

If you want to travel among the stars and enhance you starseededness, then you need to become more powerful mental beings. That is the basis for interplanetary travel. Also, it is part of the basis of ascension because you must mentally understand the concept to be able to participate in it. Using mental energy is a way you can more directly experience the Creator without endangering your ego consciousness or losing yourselves. If you have not mastered the mental energy, then the ecstasy achieved through the emotions can result in psychological damage.

It is within your grasp to be able to use your mental energy to move interdimensionally and to move out of the solar system. How can you move out of the solar system in your emotional bodies? It would be very difficult. However, your mental body can take you out of the solar system and return you safely. You have the ability. Now it is just a matter of education. It is a matter of proper mental conceptions and alignments. Believing involves the participation of your emotional bodies. It is here that your emotional bodies deter the ability of the mental body by doubting.

Emotional energy can be the most confusing and the most dangerous. It can bring you to the highest planes, even if you are unprepared. You can go to higher planes emotionally and not understand how it is affecting you mentally. This is something that would be intolerable to us.

Many people have had negative experiences in their previous incarnations. Generally, it is correct that previous patterns, or blocks, from other lifetimes need to be an unlocked and released. Equally important, however, is the teaching process. Some are so involved in releasing that they are not doing the starseed work—working to heal others and working to heal the planet. All lightworkers and starseeds need to balance personal releasing with educating and healing others.

It is not necessary to release everything negative before beginning your mission. You can use mental energy to find shortcuts for clearing some of the old karmic patterns. You can release trauma without reliving it, for example. Hypnotic trance work also can be used. There will be a growing awareness of how to use your guides more directly in hypnosis, and how to use out-of-body travel to integrate and release emotional blockages.

NEGATIVE IMPLANTS

Negative implants are thought patterns or beliefs that control or restrict the natural flow of consciousness. They exist as real energy patterns. We know you have read of this problem with negative implants—the Kryon energy and others who are trying to use thought-control implants. This has been occurring even on a governmental basis where they are trying to implant different energies into you. You must be free of all negative implants in order to access the natural, heightened consciousness that is your birthright.

We ask you to become aware of all implants that are of a negative source. We ask you to release all implants that are not providing you health, happiness, and progress in your evolution as a planetary being. This is an extremely important exercise for all who wish to be cleansed, for all who wish to be centered. You are continuously bombarded with implants from your television, from your political arena and many other sources too numerous to list. As you hear our words, as you are etherically brought aboard our ships, know that all negative implants not in your highest good will be released. You are expanding your mind-brain energy. Free from negative implants, your intelligence can be in equilibrium so that you are fresh, vibrant, creative, and stable.

We know that some of you are struggling with your emotional bodies, but as you release other implants that are of a negative nature, you will find that your emotional bodies are also going to seek a new stabilization, a new harmony.

We are confident that you will continue this process of discharge. You need to release and be clear of negative implants. You have everything within you to know how to proceed, and how to process this clearing. You do not need a direction from an exterior source to tell you what to do, because all the codes are within you, and can be easily accessed as you continue to raise your vibration.

We are sending light to your crown chakra. We wish to activate your crown chakras. It is a high frequency light that is bursting into your energy system. Feel this bright blue light coming very intensely into your crown. This blue light is coming from a source on our spiritual healing center that we can telepathically transmit to you. It is like food to your intelligence, for your brain. Whatever problem you may have, you will still be able to access this new energy and new light.

Negative implants are also being used by extraplanetary beings. Some extraterrestrials do want to control you. The Arcturians, however, want you to be free. We are here to help you become completely free of external control. You have a special energy, and as you develop your consciousness and galactic presence, you will be able to reach out and explore in different ways because of the perspective you are developing on the Earth. We are enjoying watching you come into your unique, planetary perspective.

Connecting with the Arcturians is going to be a way of stabilizing your clarity, even protecting your consciousness, enabling you to move to a higher consciousness. We are concerned at the heightened level of mind control that is now occurring, and the way that you are being exposed to different levels of mind control. Rest assured that you will be protected. You can also protect yourselves through higher awareness and other ways that you will soon discover.

It would be most appropriate to have direct work done by a specialized healer for the removal of negative implants. The healer should do tones and sounds and project intense light, love, and energy to the person involved. You can view the implant as a tick stuck to your etheric self. Through much light and sound, the tick, or implant, then has to let go of its grasp.

A new implant is not what you need. Rather, more light, love, and a heightened energy vibration is exactly what you need to loosen and free yourself of old implants. We hope that many people will hear these words about the removal of negative implants. This is a very important aspect concerning all of the healing work being done on your planet at this time.

We are very connected to the music of Mozart. Many of you will sense our presence while listening to the beautiful work that he did, bringing so much light to the planet. If Mozart's music is listened to for a period of forty eight to ninety six hours, the vibrations will help to dissolve negative implants.

Take advantage of the higher clarity that is going to come to all of you. It is a time for all on the planet who can connect with us to move into greater clarity about what you are doing here, and how you are functioning. Be as conscious as you can. All of you who hear our words from Arcturus, know that this is your great gift, and do not let anyone negatively implant your consciousness. You be the director of your consciousness. This is what you need in order to make the next series of evolutionary changes that are about to occur.

HUMAN MENTAL CAPACITIES

One of your present limitations is that you do not have a high level of mental concentration. Currently, the human race does not have great abilities to concentrate. Only a few of you have shown a strong ability to concentrate. It is forthcoming, however, for many of you. We will work with you, and teach you how to be great concentrators. The ascension is an effort in concentration. It is an effort in focusing. Healing sounds can deepen your level of concentration and deepen your level of multidimensional activation.

Your mental capacities are going to become intensified. You will be pleased at your abilities to work mentally. There has been a lot of confusion about the mental body. Some believe that the mental body should be suspended during ascension so that the emotional body can come through. We can tell you that the arrangement of your mental body is one of the most beautiful arrangements in the galaxy.

The abilities of your mental body are vast. The mental body's ability to relate to the emotional body is being intensely studied. Many of the extraterrestrials are very interested in how you go about doing that. Unfortunately, many of you on your planet are not even attempting to relate the two bodies, even though it is your unique birthright and ability to have these bodies work together. You will find that it is the emotional body that is hindering the development of the mental body despite the fact that some feel that it is the other way around.

We are particularly interested in working with you on developing your mental bodies and your thought patterns and projections. One of our specialties is using thought projections to help overcome barriers in your third-dimensional densities.

THE CONCEPT OF FREE WILL

Free will is a concept that you have on the third dimension. It is part of the training that you must go through on the third dimension. Free will implies that you do not know the outcome. You do something, and you think the result will end up one way, but you do not know for sure.

If we were to come into the third dimension with you, we would not define our actions as partaking of free will, because we could see immediately all of the consequences of our actions. From our perspective then, what we have described of us coming into your dimension would not be free will, because we would not choose something to do that would be harmful.

This concept of free will does not make sense on the fifth dimension. Do not try to carry it over from the third because you will become totally confused. It is not the same life. You do things with total knowing on the fifth. On the third, you are living in the dark. Even those of you who are choosing to live as spiritually as possible do not know the outcome.

CHAPTER 6

THE HUMAN SUBCONSCIOUS

W̲e want to work with you on the very important subject of the human subconscious and the relationship of the subconscious to the ascension process. The subconscious activates the ascension codes that reside within your DNA. The subconscious can be defined in your terms as a computer in this sense. Certain functions are "programmed," and therefore the outcome can be predicted. It is important for you to understand the control that you can have if you work through the laws of the subconscious mind.

You do not yet comprehend the vastness of your subconscious. You may think that you have a handle on it, but your handle is but a small one. Your subconscious extends into other dimensions. Your subconscious does relate to your other coexisting lifetimes. Your culture, however, has closed off that aspect of your subconscious. Therefore, you have been denied, through cultural training, the ability to go into those realms. This is all changing now, as we come to the transformation of the ascension.

You are awakening to your starseed connection. All of these things are helping you to open to the vastness of your existence. Do not believe for a moment that it is confined as you may think, or that you are living a simple life and following simple patterns. You are simultaneously living multi-layers, and you can come into a heightened, transforming awareness of yourselves by activating your subconscious to open to all realms. You can even open to the fifth-dimensional realm.

Yes, you are transforming at this moment. This transformation is indicated by your energy alignments and by your directing yourselves spiritually. You are preparing. You have been working on your subconscious in preparation for the ascension for at least three to four years. Many of you have worked on this through readings, group discussions, and by your connecting with us and other ascended masters. These are all inputs into your subconscious.

The subconscious is helping to manifest your ascension. We already see changes in your structures. We see your openings and your reaching out. You have new links into the fifth dimension. You have been programming your computer subconscious, and it is time to heighten the input. When we are working with the subconscious, we will use terms now as if it were a computer. It is time to increase your personal programming so that you will be closer to manifesting this outcome, the outcome being the entry into the fifth dimension.

As we see how close you are to a transformation, we ask you if you sense your closeness to us. If you sense your changes, and if you sense that you have been reprogramming so much these past several years, then you are getting ready for the "payoff." We think that it is important for you to improve and increase your personal programming even though you have been working so hard and focusing your energy on the ascension. You will need to increase your work—increase your mental, emotional, and spiritual activity. You have to make up for several incarnations in some cases. We will increase our work with you at the same time.

We have purified our subconscious minds. Once a core group among our race committed themselves to the transformation of Arcturus and of our people, it became easy to embark on the purification of the Arcturians. This was successfully completed many eons ago.

Let us bring in the blue light again from the Arcturians. Observe this blue light from the star Arcturus and let this blue light come into your subconscious. This is a new variation of light, for we have worked before with the golden light in your subconscious mind. Now the blue light will coat your subconscious mind. In this position, you have the ability to inject an infusion of light into the subconscious of the human race. You are powerful starseeds. You are powerful as dimensional travelers. You are powerful because you are now in a position to implement a new program, or perspective, into the planetary subconscious. We are helping you to deploy that program by infusing blue light through your subconscious into the whole planetary subconscious of the Earth.

Computer technology is obviously important for the development of your species. We wish to recommend that people explore this link with the computer and with the subconscious mind. There have been TV programs and movies that have explored the link with the subconscious, but they have intentionally projected this relationship in a negative way. Know that exactly the opposite can happen. The computer can make more sense of the human subconscious, and help you interact with it and study it. When we want to interact with the computer, we project our thought to the computer. Telepathy is actually talking to another person. You must understand this. It is not just having a thought. You still have to direct the thought. If you wanted to send a thought to someone, you must talk to him or her in your mind.

TELEPATHY AND THE SUBCONSCIOUS MIND

The subconscious mind provides the medium for the transfer of thoughts in the third dimension. The human subconscious and the universal subconscious is an energy field that exists throughout your dimension. Thoughts can be sent out through subconscious wavelengths.

Sending thoughts is easier then receiving them. We are obviously more concerned with your ability to receive our thoughts. We can read your thoughts. We can read what you are sending us. This is not a problem. We do not read thoughts that you do not want to have read. Many people think that if you are telepathic then you know everything of what the person is thinking. This is true, but with telepathy comes a responsibility. Thoughts can be tagged.

Tagging thoughts can be compared to creating files on your computer. Private thoughts can be tagged like personal files in a computer. If there are thoughts that you want to hide, then you can tag them as private and then we will not interact with those thoughts. We understand your development and we do not judge you for wanting to hide certain thoughts. It is still your right. We are not in the business of finding out things about you that you do not want us to know.

You can also communicate emotion telepathically. You direct, for example, love, and then you send the love. You can send fear as well. Some of the extraterrestrials, specifically the Grays, as you refer to them, have sent thoughts of fear to many people on the Earth. Extraterrestrial beings can enter your subconscious. The Grays, for example, felt that they could enter the whole race because they were tapping into the planetary subconscious. Fortunately, you are providing a counterbalance to that energy, because you are allowing a higher frequency to be focused into the planetary subconscious—that is, an energy of light, love, expansion, and spiritual light.

Unlocking Codes through the Subconscious

We would like to return to the concept of the codes for a moment. The codes are in your mind and are telling you how to respond. One example of a simple code would be stopping at a red light. This becomes embedded in your mind. There are deeper codes that are locked within your subconscious that stop you from understanding and experiencing other multidimensional lives. These codes prevent you from experiencing your dimensional expansiveness. But you can reprogram the subconscious to unlock these codes.

From our perspective, the codes were locked by those beings that wanted to control the Earth and by those forces that wanted to subvert the people of Earth. You could say that the codes are locked, but you also could say that it is programmed in you to ignore the codes. That is the same as locking, is it not? You still cannot get in.

You can access the higher dimensional realms by unlocking these same codes. You can hear certain words, and when they are said with the right intention, they will serve to remind you to open to this higher energy. The opening of the codes must be done through the subconscious mind, and that is why many prayers use repetition. Repeated prayers or affirmations can unlock these codes in your subconscious mind.

We like some of the words that have been given to you for unlocking the codes, such as *Kadosh, Kadosh, Adonai Tsevaot*. We have heard these words before through Metatron. It is not necessary to understand the meaning of each word. He granted the power of those words to be associated with the opening of light within your subconscious. You can receive this light through your subconscious mind. You have been receiving light externally, so to speak, through your crown chakra. With this information we are giving you now, you can unlock the codes, and you can receive light from within. Your subconscious can provide an inner light for you. Feel that inner light coming up now.

Our healing chambers work to organize your thought patterns in a way that brings a sense of harmony and peace to you. We have found it most effective to work with you first through your thoughts, and then we will send emotional energy in the healing chambers. Once your codes are unlocked, you have all the apparatus to work with all the frequencies in the galaxy and in the universe. It is not really a matter of teaching you, because you already have this ability. It is more a matter of unlocking the codes to allow this interface. We send you the inner light, and we will assist you in activating your subconscious to bring in light from within. This is your next step.

CLEANSING THE SUBCONSCIOUS

The subconscious contains many dense energy patterns that have been placed there. The negative aliens, the animalistic evolutionary process you have come through, and the culture itself have all contributed to the negative aspects of your subconscious. To move you to the next realm, it is clear that you must purify your subconscious minds. The subconscious is a beautiful aspect, but it has been polluted from the sources that we have mentioned. The beauty of your subconscious is that it can be purified.

If you ask, we will send you a purifying, golden light that will activate a cleansing. Your affirmation should be: "I cleanse my subconscious." That is all you need to say when using the golden rays from the Arcturians. You carry with you the wounds and emotional scars from other incarnations, and from your current lifetime, as well. We are not telling you that you will be totally cleansed from these wounds and scars. But we are saying that we can help to cleanse your subconscious. Then we will be able to work with you in an even more accelerated way. Nothing can prevent you from moving to higher consciousness once your subconscious has been properly aligned and cleansed of negative patterns.

Your subconscious mind will help you to focus on and practice all activities and thoughts that promote your transformation into the fifth dimension. We have a beautiful affirmation for you: "All thoughts and patterns that are not serving a higher purpose are hereby discarded and removed." Your subconscious mind will then open to experience interdimensional energy, communications, and even travel, as well. This is a very important affirmation, for this opening needs to be activated now in your subconscious mind. You will then be able to move yourselves into this higher realm.

This subconscious cleansing purification should be practiced regularly for seven days. Each day you should spend, at least, twenty minutes to a half an hour cleansing the subconscious. Just like you practice juice fasts for digestive cleansing, now you must do a cleansing for the subconscious. When you cleanse your body, you do not give up your body. Cleansing removes "dirt." It does not remove the good parts.

Call in the golden light from the Arcturians, and use the affirmations that we have stated. Do this for seven days. You should become aware of a lightness about you, and of a blue glow or blue halo around you. This is simply a sign of a cleansed subconscious mind.

It is our observation that you are very susceptible to damaging your subconscious. This is not being said judgmentally. You are living in a very difficult time, in an evolutionary time that is still connected with a great deal of animalistic, subconscious energy. Being here on Earth, you will need to work on subconscious cleansing continually. But after the initial seven-day cleansing, you will not need to work on this as intently, perhaps two or three minutes each day. You should also continue to reinforce the thought that you will now be open to interdimensional energy, communication, and travel.

It is true that many lightworkers are lost and unconscious because there has not been a cleansing of their subconscious. These lightworkers have not actively worked at releasing their accumulated negative patterns and thoughtforms. Many young people, however, are now coming into this energy. It is true that there are more people who need to be activated because so many are still asleep.

You need to increase messages to your subconscious mind, increase the light, increase the unlocking of the codes, and increase your connections with us. It is really a time of great acceleration. You have been in training to increase your energy. You have been preparing for this. You must not waste this opportunity. You are close to making a big leap, a big move. You have successfully placed parts of yourself into the fifth dimension. You can envision it as a lake, and you are "popping up" to the surface.

You are accomplishing something extremely important when then you program your subconscious to allow a higher spiritual light to come in, and also to send out love, light, and expansion into the world. Our mission is to assist in the spiritual and dimensional transformation of the planet and of the whole human race. We are asking you to increase your work and increase the directions to your subconscious mind. You must work to unlock even more. It may seem like a lot to ask, but you have the foundation to do this. It will not be difficult for you.

We send love to you. Know that this love that we send you is placed into your subconscious now.

CHAPTER 7

CONNECTING WITH
THE ARCTURIANS

We want to speak to you about connecting with us, for working with us can be very helpful to you. First, you must understand that in order to interact with us and other beings from different dimensions, you must create a space for us in your mind, your heart, and your spirit. You must have an opening that allows us to occupy this space. That includes the space within your belief systems.

Next, you must clear yourself of earthly concerns. Many have asked how to move to a higher dimension as an Earth being. The answer is simple: You must do a clearing of the earthly mindset, a clearing of your attachments and entanglements. Attachments are so powerful that many of you resist physical death to the point where it is painful. They are so powerful that some of you cannot remember that you have been in different dimensions in other lifetimes.

You can go to other dimensions in the dream state. You can also accomplish this through trance meditation. Moving to another dimensional state consciously requires that you do clearings. Prepare yourself by making an open space for us. You must also remove the possibility that factors from your attachment selves will intervene. We are not criticizing your attachment to the Earth plane. It is normal. As an inhabitant of planet Earth, it is your reality. This is where your etheric cord has its roots.

If you could see auras, you would see many etheric roots projected from your auric field into the Earth. Through meditation you can remove those roots and project them higher into the galaxy. Try that exercise now. Remove several of the projected roots that are entangling you to the Earth. Allow them to be projected upward and then you will be able to open up more to the energies that we are bringing down to you. We want you to focus on allowing your spirit auras to leave your physical bodies and spiral upward. Your physical bodies will remain in your chairs. You can spiral upward using thought projection.

We will work with you on an interdimensional plane. What does that mean? Interdimensional actually means between dimensions. It is a way station, since you are not yet in the next dimension. To come into the fifth dimension, you have to cut the etheric cords that are attached to the third dimension.

Connections are so important in all galactic consciousness. You are already connected telepathically with many beings. When you are able to connect with one source, soon you will move easily into connecting with other sources. It is the initial connection with a new source that is the most important. Once you do that, your electromagnetic field will be permanently set up for receiving communications from that source.

You will know you have arrived in interdimensional space when you can contact us directly, as opposed to through a channel. We are seeking to meet you in the interdimensional realm. Many of the things we teach you cannot be accomplished in the Earth realm. When you are in third-dimensional space, you cannot perfect thought projection. In order to project thoughts more effectively, you must come into a higher realm.

We are asking you now to project yourselves into the fifth dimension and to the interdimensional plane. This will make it easier for you when the time comes to meet us and your guides. Do not simply wait for the ascension to happen. Do not simply wait to be "beamed up," as many of you have called this process. Dimensional travel is a process that begins before it happens. It is a continual process. Begin working on it now.

We can, under certain circumstances, manifest in your dimension, but it is a difficult process that requires scientific accuracy. Were we to calculate inaccurately, then we could trap the being who was sent to your dimension. Because of the risk, it is not always safe for us to manifest. Moreover, it is to your advantage to meet us interdimensionally. One of our missions is to encourage you to move into interdimensional space. Through thought projection, we can send down an auric presence of ourselves rather than sending our actual physical presence.

ANCHORING THE ARCTURIAN ENERGY

We on the Arcturian system are very tuned into your soul missions, and we are coming here by direction from many of the White Brotherhood/Sisterhood to assist you, and remind you that your soul mission is important. You need to remind yourself of your mission, and part of that mission is your ability to anchor and connect with the energy we send to you now. You are going to help your planet to connect with the Arcturian energy.

The Arcturian energy is a bright sun energy that is coming to the planet, and it is in alignment with the Savior energy. It is bringing a force, an awakening energy, and you who are working with us now are the forerunners of this energy. You are the planters of this energy. You know how important it is to bring down this new force. Open your hearts now, for this is the place where the new energy is going to be anchored in your body. Receive the violet-gold flame that is being beamed down to you from our ship.

Our ship is above the planet, and we have several other ships that are throughout the country at this time. They are coordinating the sending of this violet-gold ray to all of the groups of forty and to all others asking to receive it. This energy is being beamed down to you now, entering into your heart chakra. From the heart, the violet-gold energy will go up and down your spinal chord. As we are speaking to you, you will find that this will be an opening, an activation, on a level that has not been experienced before by you.

SPIRITUAL TRUTH

This is Sananda. My dear ones, you are all so beautiful in your spiritual array. I know you are eager to come to the next realm. I am overseeing many different paths that are being made available to you. The Arcturian path, for instance, is a high path of pure consciousness. I want you to understand that your essence, your spirit, is really defined as pure consciousness, not as your physical body. It is the expansion of your consciousness that will help you to enter the fifth dimension.

The Arcturians are not only guardians of pure spirit but are actual soul masters who guide souls into the higher realms. Many of you wish to know when you can totally enter the fifth dimension. Many of you are ready to give up the physical plane life and enter into the gardens, come to the higher dimensional planets, live on Arcturus, or travel to the Pleiades. I can only tell you that your time for coming here is very near. Even though I will not give you a date, I can assure you that you are on the very edge of this great evolutionary process on the Earth.

The consciousness of the masses on the planet has shifted tremendously. Your hearts are more open, and your ability to love is much greater. You are able to sense the love we have for you. Your participation in a group format will help to move the consciousness of the whole Adamic race. Therefore, it is very important that you hold this evolutionary consciousness, as well as implant and anchor this higher consciousness on the Earth. This is a sacred task and a sacred mission. Our Arcturian friends are helping to stabilize the planet, and they are guiding many into the path of ascension. This is Sananda.

We wish to speak to you now about the transmission of spiritual truth. We wish to share with you our knowledge about spiritual development. Once we transmit this to you, then you can use this knowledge to magnify your progress, assimilate your lessons, and progress very quickly up the corridors. This is the way of the universe. This is the way of growth and expansion. Spiritual truth has always been transmitted from the higher realms.

There have been many cases where religious leaders have gone out into the wilderness to receive these transmissions. There is no reason now with your development, why you could not now be at the same intensity. Activate your light within through healing sounds and identification with higher beings, such as ourselves, such as the Pleiadians and Sananda-Jesus. Sananda-Jesus came from the galactic Central Sun. His birth was through a beam of light directly from the galactic core carrying his spirit to Earth. It was a monumental moment.

By the act of identifying with the masters and the higher beings, you become a part of them. You place your presence in a merged state with them, and this brings you to their spiritual level. You can, and should, identify with more than one master or teacher. Each brings a unique vibration, or perspective, that can help you in your understanding of spiritual truth.

Along with Sananda-Jesus and others, we ask you to also merge or identify with the Arcturians. Take yourself, take your consciousness, and let it come up your crown chakra, up to a ship that is over the planet. Each of you has an Arcturian waiting for you. You can come up to be with them, and they will merge with you. You have heard of walk-ins, and you have always thought of them coming down into your consciousness. But you can also beam your consciousness up to us. We can allow you to be part of us temporarily. You can bring your consciousness to one of us and experience the Arcturian perspective. All is energy. All is electromagnetic vibration. You are moving, transforming. You are preparing your energy field to receive an energy infusion that will allow you to project yourselves to the realm of the fifth dimension.

SPIRITUAL ENERGY

We are always pleased to know that other powerful teachers and guides are coming to interact with you. The White Brotherhood/Sisterhood and the angelic presences have been very active in supporting your work with us and giving us permission to work with you. There are other beings in the galaxy, beings that come from Antares, some from the higher Sirian energy, and beings from the Pleiades who work with us. There are beings from stars that you are not aware of by name, like the Low-koos. The Low-koos star system is approximately 1,580 light years from Earth. There are other beings from the sixth dimension who are also entering the interdimensional corridors that some of you have created.

The universal law of energy is such that spiritual energy attracts very powerfully. It is the most powerful attractive force in the universe—spiritual energy and spiritual love. Enjoy the many beings present that are working with you. These beings can pierce the densities of your third dimension. But the question is whether you, who are actually living in the dense environment, can receive, process, and interpret these higher energy frequencies.

We will give you several tones and sounds that will attune you to some of those energies now that are coming into you (the channel tones several unique sounds). This energy is a refined frequency that has to do with a lightness in both physical weight and light energy.

This specialized energy that is coming into you now is very delicate and intricate.

Let the energy come into your crown chakra as blue light. This is a special, dimensionally synthesized frequency of energy that is coming to you now, and it going to help you to receive and process frequencies from other higher dimensional beings. You have to be attuned to these frequencies. It is very important that you work to tune yourself so that you can be a proper receiver and a transmitter of this light to others.

A New Awareness

You are experiencing a period of new energy balancing. The new energy is very powerful, and many people are finding the new equilibrium difficult to adjust to. Know that this equilibrium is going to be one in which you will be able to access more electromagnetic energy. It is important for all of you to understand that you are electromagnetic beings. It is important for you to maintain a balance between the positive and negative and at all times seek a harmony between the two forces in your energy fields.

All of your technology and all the new breakthroughs that you have developed in the past thirty to forty years are based on electromagnetic field vibrations. This is no coincidence, because you are electromagnetic beings. You are seeking to mimic your own brain systems. But you will also find that you can accomplish much personal growth by internally accelerating your electromagnetic fields. You will be able to access and utilize your full intelligence.

The Arcturian healing energy allows us to be in a state of resonance with the galactic source. We are able to connect to a higher galactic energy source that, when you become a receptor, will greatly help you to bring yourself into a better energy balance and enhance your intelligence. This will not only help you to become clear in all that you are doing in your daily work and thinking processes, but also it will help you to resonate and vibrate with the higher energy that is now available on your planet.

Indeed, your soul is evolving. You have received the knowledge that your soul is eternal, but you should also understand that everything that is eternal is also evolving. Massive expansion occurs as part of the natural course of universe progression. We, the Arcturians, are also expanding, just as you are expanding in your consciousness.

We know that you are galactic in source. The energies that brought you to this planet originated from outside your solar system. This is why, as you are accelerating in this evolutionary state, you will now be able to comfortably access your extrasolar, extraplanetary origins.

YOUR MULTIDIMENSIONAL SELVES

We want you to become aware of your multidimensional selves. Understand that this self that you are now experiencing in this Earth incarnation is but one aspect of your multidimensional self. You are getting only a glimpse of who you are. You are much greater than what you are experiencing in this manifestation. At the same time, what you are experiencing in this manifestation is truly a reflection of your greater self. You do have access to many gifts from your multidimensional self.

Your multidimensional self is already connected to us. It is this multidimensional self that has had contact with us before, and feels very comfortable with us. It is a matter of bringing down the different aspects of your higher self into a consciousness that you can work with here on the Earth plane. We want you to bring this energy down into your awareness. Let us give you an example. Since you have a multidimensional self, part of you can already be working on one of our ships. In another sense, part of you can already be visiting Arcturus, while part of you is coming to our healing chambers. We are working with many of you in your sleep state. Your higher self has given us permission for this.

We want to help you activate this transition of introducing the multidimensional self and bringing it down into your consciousness so that you can access it. We know you are very interested in becoming a powerful being on the Earth. The way to become a powerful being on Earth is to bring down the as pects of self that are more etheric and multidimensional. You can do it. In meditation, we want you to open the gate of your consciousness to your multidimensional self. For it is that multidimensional connection that enables you to connect with us. You see, we are a transition, we are a conduit for you.

You can connect to us with your multidimensional senses. Open the multidimensional gate to your higher self. The multidimensional aspect brings you into our corridor—an Arcturian corridor of light. You can access your psychic abilities, bilocation, clairvoyance, telepathy, channeling, and visioning. Those psychic traits are often identified with Earth matters, but today, we want you to use your psychic abilities to go into your multidimensional self. You can ask for Arcturian guides to work with you.

We would now ask you to participate in an exercise with us. Lift yourself up to a place now over the Earth, where we will all connect. In this higher state, envision a pyramid. Focus your attention on the pyramid. Now bring your consciousness to a point on top of the pyramid. From that point, feel your consciousness separating from the physical body and from even the etheric body. We are now moving as a collective consciousness. From this point on the top of the pyramid, in collective consciousness with us, travel down a long, beautiful, light-filled tunnel. It is a corridor to the fifth dimension.

Place your consciousness now in the Arcturian guide that has been assigned to you. You can venture out into an aspect of the fifth dimension by putting your consciousness into the guide that has been assigned to you. Step out! Look through the eyes of your guide. You are inside a very highly trained being. You are inside an Arcturian. Feel, see, taste, experience this dimension. Your Arcturian guide can also connect to your multidimensional self. By raising the crown chakra energy within the Arcturian guide (it is like an antenna), you can suddenly receive many different instructions, pieces of information about yourself. This information can come into your consciousness from the "antenna" of the Arcturian guide. If you have participated in this meditation, the information is now being transferred to you.

We want you to continue to experience this fifth-dimensional light. You will not, however, be able to stay there long, for there are limitations of the Arcturian host that you have come into. We ask you to step back with the Arcturian guide, who is stepping back now back into the tunnel. From the tunnel, we will begin to withdraw and we will travel back through the tunnel, back into the point of the pyramid where we started, back to where your consciousness departed. Bring your consciousness back to the pyramid now. From that point at the top of the pyramid, allow your consciousness to descend back into your etheric body. It is very important to return the same way you left. This is very important for the re-integration process. Now return to your physical body on Earth. Let this happen gently and smoothly, and enjoy it, for you are now connected to your multidimensional selves.

The transfer of your consciousness is the key to moving to the next dimension. As you begin to become more comfortable with that fact, you will be able to move more easily. Develop your ability to dematerialize. We know that this sounds outrageous to you. But can you understand that ascension is a form of dematerialization? The body follows the mind. The mind follows the consciousness.

You have learned a valuable lesson today in how the ascension will work—by dematerialization. We recommend you practice this type of exercise. When the ascension occurs, you will not have time to go through steps, such as in the meditation we just experienced. Know that the ascension will be instantaneous.

ENERGY ALIGNMENTS

It is important to understand the significance of energy alignments. Alignments occur on all multidimensional levels. You have many levels of physical alignments. You have spiritual alignments with your various bodies, including the emotional, mental, and physical. Human beings also have alignments with the energies of the Earth. However, because of the energy shifts now occurring and the overwhelming abuse of the planetary systems, it is easy to be out of alignment with the Earth energies.

Alignments of the solar system also affect you when certain planets come into alignment with each other. Then there are the other solar systems in the galaxy that you are not aware of. You can also attune to the alignments in different sectors of the galaxy. There are inner, middle, and outer sectors of the galaxy in the same way that there are inner, middle, and outer planets in your solar system. Your solar system represents a miniature model of the galaxy. Thus, you can understand from our presentation that there are alignments within alignments and so forth.

Humans experience energy alignments with the sister stars and binary stars as well. These alignments occur on a longterm basis, and are difficult to measure from Earth's standpoint because of the shortness of your physical lifetimes.

Each of these alignments is powerful. You may use energy alignments or you may ignore them. The choice is yours. An alignment is an opportunity to grow, expand, and experience unity on a new level. You have an opportunity to experience a new unity when you are able to bring yourself into alignment physically, emotionally, and mentally. You are constantly on a spiral that offers opportunities for new energy alignments with new information and new awarenesses. Since you are not always aware of the multidimensional planes, these alignments are important because they can help you to integrate and gain awareness of the different dimensions.

You might be stuck, inhibited by the linear nature of your density. However, at each new alignment, you can transcend the density by taking the opportunity to experience a portion of your multidimensional existence.

The first step in using alignments is to be aware of them. You can induce the effects of alignments by understanding that they are points of acceleration. Focus your awareness on the Earth, the solar system, the galaxy, and then beyond the field of galaxies. The galaxies themselves come into alignment with the various universes. This is a concept that is difficult for many to understand—namely that universes can come into alignment with another energy field. We are still seeking ways to understand and explain it.

Continuing along this line of awareness brings you back to yourselves. It is within yourselves that you can bring this energy into alignment. You may choose to bring an internal alignment into your hearts, blood systems, cellular structures, or genetic codes. You can return to those who placed the codes within the human genetic makeup and learn about their energy and awareness. The information of the galaxies and of the universes is already in your genetic coding. This is why many of you are such strong seekers of the great cosmic picture.

BOUNCING

Let us get more "down to Earth." You have particular energies that you need to comprehend. These alignments will be of assistance to you. You are in a period, from our perspective, of "bouncing." It is a time of dramatic shifts back and forth. Some describe it as being on a ship out on a stormy sea. Some might become seasick if they are unable to return to a center position. Those who are in alignment can rise above this phenomenon and look at the bouncing.

The planet is seeking a new alignment. This is what we believe the ascension is about. When a planet seeks a new balance, a phase of awkwardness is experienced. The old system becomes top heavy, but it is still very powerful. The old thought patterns become more tenacious. This means that as the shifting continues, those in control on your planet are seeking to bear down and hold on to these old patterns and structures. Does this not tell you how you should respond? The more you hold on, the more you will be thrown around. If you let go, you can rise above the situation and observe.

When you let go, then you truly become a master like Sananda-Jesus. From our perspective, one of his lessons was that of letting go, even at the moment of death. We are not suggesting that you will have to go through such a dramatic episode, but when you start from what would be the worst possible outcome, perhaps the rest becomes easier. When you learn to rise above the situation, a new stability will occur on your planet. The more of you who can detach and rise in dimensional perspective, the easier it will be to create a new balance on the Earth.

Many have asked about what they can do to prevent imbalances. When you rise, as we have explained, and focus your thoughts and your love on a higher perspective, then you can affect a change. From that perspective, you can send love to the roots of the Earth.

OPENING THE CROWN CHAKRA

This is Juliano, and we are the Arcturians. When we look at each of you, we see that each has a certain vibration, or level of energy, around your crown chakra. This crown chakra is your central receptor for universal energy. It is also interesting that this area is mostly blocked, because you have not been trained from childhood to use this energy center. You have not been brought up with that center open.

We, on Arcturus, are very pleased at the attention that is paid to developing the crown chakra on our planet, and the ability to connect with universal energy. However, connecting to universal energy through your crown chakra is still a new experience for you. You must be reminded about the crown chakra and its connection by having all blocks around this energy center removed. We can use sound to help you bring your crown chakra into alignment.

It will be a different experience for you to have your crown chakra totally open. Many of you have focused on working on your heart chakra and your third eye. Now it is time to direct your energy to the crown chakra. You have been doing this light work for enough years that you will find it easier for your crown chakra to be brought into alignment.

Take a moment to focus your consciousness on your crown chakra. Your crown chakra should be very wide open now. We ask you now to leave your body and project your consciousness to an interdimensional Arcturian ship in the Jupiter corridor. You are now sitting in a room similar to our library; you connected to this place through your crown chakra. You can look far below and begin to see your crown chakra down on Earth. It is wide open!

We will give you information through your crown chakra. This information will be related to the energy and knowledge that you need to assimilate for your mission. Each of you has a specific aspect of this work on the third dimension that needs to be completed. Perhaps there are certain people that you need to work with, or certain ideas or knowledge that you need to bring forth to others. We will work with you in order to bring this knowledge to you through your crown chakra. We are allowing a permanent connection from your crown chakra to this library on our interdimensional ship. There are so many questions that you need to have answered and resolved.

Now we will go beyond the Jupiter corridor. You are sitting on the ship as your etheric self. We ask you to once again connect to your crown chakra in order to go out of the solar system, and travel to the Arcturian Temple of Tomar to experience the crystal light. Know that the light from this crystal is a perfected light specially designed to help you incorporate the Arcturian frequency into your third-dimensional reality.

We are giving you a special light ray from the temple that will emit a particular frequency you can use in third-dimensional life. You not only need this thread of light that is coming, but you need to have confidence in this connection. Let it come into your crown chakra and then into the crown chakra of the Earth. Observe that we are in three parts now. The bottom layer is residing on the Earth; the second is in your body inside the interdimensional ship near Jupiter; the third is your other body in the Arcturian Temple of Tomar. Let all three of the crown chakras connect.

We are aligning our frequency generator, our crystal light, specifically to your abilities to receive it. We are sending a golden light down through all three bodies. The third-dimensional body on Earth will experience a warmth, a bursting of love, an angelic surge of love coming down all three bodies into your Earth body. Archangel Michael wishes to speak to you at this time.

This is Archangel Michael. I am pleased that you understand that the Arcturian frequency is a frequency of higher vibration and higher love. I know you have heard me speak so much about cutting the chords of attachment. It is also important for you to be a conduit for this connection, because we need to solidify and to hold the Earth dimension together. This has been a mission of great angelic presence. We have been working to assist you and your planet in many ways.

I have a message for you that concerns the fulfillment of your work. We are able, through the grace and power of Sananda, to offer you a special boost for your evolutionary process. I am going to ask each of you to bring back with you what it is you need to happen to make your life easier. I want you to ask for that, and when you come back into your body, I will then assist you energetically. Whatever it is that you need now to have come to fruition to make your life easier, ask now for that to occur on this level with the Arcturians. When we return to the third-dimensional body, we will continue this process.

Be very clear that what you are asking for is what you really need. The reason why we are offering this is because we understand how important this work is that you are doing. The predicaments and blocks that you experience can be easily resolved so that you can dedicate more of your energy to the mission of connecting to the fifth dimension. This is Archangel Michael.

This is Juliano. We do take an interest in your personal problems and we want to assist you. We also work with the angelic forces that are so close to you. With this connection, with this light, we ask you now to return to the second level. From the second level, please slowly return to the first. Leave the interdimensional library on the ship, and come back into your body at this time. Even though you have come back, we want you to maintain this connection to the third level, to the crystal light in the Arcturian Temple of Tomar. This connection will remain open this evening for your dreamtime.

CHAPTER 8

THE NEED FOR HEALING

Healing is very important to you now as you go through the transition of releasing attachments. You are releasing some of the early life history that you have had on the planet, even though you continue to maintain an interaction with those past energies. The key to healing lies in interacting with those energies, including both past-life energy and energy from childhood wounds. The energies should become fluid. They are part of your history and being. The experiences you have had on the planet are all relevant. You are seeking a unity, an integration of all of those energies. They will remain a part of your new integration. Once you understand them, you will be able to interact with the energies and they will not dominate you. You will then become unstuck.

We are following many of you all of the time. We are connected with you directly when you call upon us. When you are not calling upon us, we do not intervene or interfere in any way with your ongoing life patterns. We will only work with you if you ask us to, and our interaction is not in interference with your karma. We will give you information, and be receptive to you when you call upon us. We are able to see all of your life patterns. We can see where you are going, what is going to develop, and how your physical bodies are going to unfold. We are very keyed in to your health. You can call on us in particular to assist you in your health developments.

We are studying how you respond to physical diseases and other physical problems. We are aware of your physical limitations. We are also aware that you will be able to transcend those limitations when you go into the higher realms. It is im portant for your own development that you learn to work within your limitations on the physical plane. However, you are all able to overcome many of the physical problems you are currently experiencing.

One aspect of our mission is to assist all of you in healing. We do healings through a method where we ask you to etherically project yourselves through a corridor and up to our ships so that we can work with you. Your health problems can be a nuisance at times, as you already know. Some of you have particularly complex health problems, yet they do not have to hinder you in your evolvement toward the goal of higher consciousness and interdimensional work. This is very important for you to understand.

We are aware of the difficulty in your immune systems that many are experiencing. Some of you already sense the compromise of your immune system. It is a challenge for you to remain in a state of health on this planet. This is again why we ask you to join us in the corridors where we are able to help you clear much of the densities and much of the negative energy that attaches to you.

New Arcturian ships have arrived in your sector of your solar system from the Arcturian area. We have brought special light ships, special healing energy, and special healers with us to assist those of you who ask for our assistance. We are serious about wanting to assist you, and we know that the most direct way is through healing. We have the technology, and we have the mental and spiritual ability to work directly with you.

We also specialize in soul regeneration. There are souls who, because of their darkness, because of their evilness and density, appear to be in a state of total annihilation. Some have speculated that these souls have been wiped out. However, we have been working on soul regeneration, including the souls of evil leaders. Souls can be regenerated through special assistance and work. It is important for those who engage in soul regeneration to be highly focused, and maintain close contact with their group soul energy. We have worked with whole groups and even with entire planets that have been annihilated through atomic weaponry or nuclear disasters. They were very much in need of soul regeneration.

HEALING ON THE ARCTURIAN SHIPS

Our healing methods have to do with aligning your frequencies and clearing all your bodies. We provide a direct connection with you by providing an interdimensional corridor, and by bringing our ships in a space over your physical presence. We send down a beam of light to help you become cleansed, feel lighter, and get in touch with yourself. We can raise your etheric self, and bring that part of you to our ship. On board, we use a healing library and healing chambers to activate and recharge your energy. You can also reconnect to earlier times and other soul lives when you are with us.

If you want to be healed on our ships, you must practice thought projection. You must be able to project yourself to the ships through thoughts. This is an important aspect. We use a highly advanced technique of meridian therapy on the ships. Rather than using pins and needles, we use our thoughts to center certain energy waves.

You are connecting to us now by reading these words. We can also give you sounds that you can work with in your meditations. We prefer to work with you in a chamber. We ask you to thought-project yourselves into the chamber, and then we can take you and the chamber up very nicely. You might conceive of the chamber as a kind of exotic phone booth. It has a circular top and you can put a chair in it or whatever you wish. You can perhaps conceive of it as even having stained glass windows. We would like you to use the sound of our name, the Arcturians, to align with us.

Some of you have had experiences on our ships, but they have not been as intense as you would have liked them to be. It requires a conscious commitment on your part to allow us to work with you. We prefer to work with you in a conscious state. You can start with a conscious request for healing, and then go to sleep, as opposed to being taken to a healing chamber during a deep sleep. We find we are able to work with you more effectively when you consciously make the commitment with your own free will. We are then able to accomplish more. We have special healing centers that use sound waves to work with the energy of your organs. Much of our healing is related to organ energy and organ problems. It is our healing specialty.

We ask you now to raise your spirit energy, come into an interdimensional corridor directly above your head, and enter the area of our ship that we call the blue room. The blue room is reserved for healing and rejuvenation. We have set aside chairs in the chamber for you. You are receiving an intense charge of blue light, a loving, spirit energy that is flowing through you now. It is magnificently warm and loving. It is activating energy for you. We have been taught by the Andromedans how to activate the blue light. We are putting more and more blue light into your auric field. It is very powerful, a blue healing energy, a telepathic form of energy.

Continue to sit in the blue room and look out at the wall in front of you. We have provided you a view of the galaxy. You can also see the different colors of the star Arcturus, which is very close now. You are looking out a special window so that you do not have to experience any harmful effects of the rays from Arcturus. This is a very powerful method of activation—to identify the star that you wish to connect with, and then the energy you need will come to you.

Know that your crown chakra is now being flooded with blue light, the light of spiritual insight. It is anchored within you. This blue light ranges from a light blue to a deep blue. It contains the light and the deep blue together. In these colors, the deep blue does not do away with the light blue. You never erase an octave, you just add to it.

The Earth vibration on the third dimension is a slower vibration. Your higher energies are steadily depleted by the third-dimensional Earth process. We know the slower vibration of the Earth and how it does draw your energy. Thus, you need to recharge as often as you can. You will need to have many more doses of this blue light in the blue chamber. You will want to continue to come back to this healing chamber. If you return to the blue healing chambers, you will eventually be able to hold a higher octave of the blue light. This is part of what you need to do for ascension—to gain a higher octave that you can stabilize. It is necessary even for us to return to the blue healing chambers in order to maintain our frequency.

PERSONAL CLEARINGS

Many of you still do not recall your commitment and your instructions before you came into the third dimension on Earth. However, it is true that you volunteered for this mission and that deep in your heart, you want to be of assistance and service in the highest possible way. Many of you are working very hard on your own personal clearings. This has to do with the resolving of your karma and personal problems. It also involves opening up your chakras and your energy fields to receive and interact with fifth-dimensional energy. It is a great challenge for many of you to balance your personal problems and the resolution of those problems with helping others and service to the Earth.

We wish to speak to all who are experiencing personal difficulties. We are concerned about your personal problems. We are sympathetic to your situation, and we have compassion for you. We know that there are not a high percentage of lightworkers on this planet. Each one of you is incredibly valuable. When you are clearer and more resolved with your personal problems, then you will be a better transmitter of this fifth-dimensional energy.

We are going to give you guidelines to assist you in clearing any energy that may be hampering you. First, open your heart chakra wider. Second, connect an energy link between your third eye and your heart. Third, mentally project a date in the future when you wish to see a complete resolution of the difficulty. This can be thirty days, fifty days, etc. Fourth, create a pathway of light from the present moment to that date that you have chosen. Fifth, when you reach that date with the pathway of light, create a resolution to your problem in your mind and project it at that point. Sixth, from that date in your projection, send an energy beam to an Arcturian ship that is in the Jupiter corridor in you solar system. By sending that beam, you are giving us permission to send energy into your pathway to assist you. Seventh, receive from us the connection from our ship to you, and this completes the energy path. Eighth, keep that energy flowing!

In many cases, your problem can be resolved by such a heightened energy and heightened perspective. When you connect your heart with your third eye, you are also able to terminate the karma that is involved in the problem you have. That moves you more quickly to a resolution. You do not need to be burdened any further. Most of the problems that you have can be resolved in a six-week period. We know that might sound phenomenal, but there are very few problems that we have seen with lightworkers that are not resolvable within six weeks.

Clearly, we cannot interfere in your karma. However, in the method that we have just described, you are in charge. You are asking us to bring an energy to you that will assist you. This is not interference. We are simply working together by your request.

TACHYON ENERGY

Tachyon energy is a pulsing energy very similar to the basic energy force of the universe. You will find the same pulsing motion in the human heart and in the auric field. The tachyon energy used in our galaxy is a force that some have compared to the universal chi energy. Tachyon healing focuses on utilizing chi, the life force. Chi energy can be placed in stones and other articles, and then transmitted into cellular structures such as the human body.

Holding tachyon energy in rocks is similar to the energy retainment found in crystals. As owners of a crystal, you can transmit your thought patterns into the crystal, which holds the thoughts as mental energy transmissions. Crystals must be cleared to remove negative thought patterns. When working with tachyon energy, however, there is no need to clear the stone, since tachyon articles sustain and generate chi energy. And unlike crystals, tachyon stones do not require programming.

Tachyon energy fulfills a need unmet by crystals for the transmutation of healing life-force energy. This life-force energy can help starseeds and healers by providing a greater unity and balance for those open to the ascension process. The tachyon stones can accelerate your spiritual work by increasing the vibratory rate of your mental and auric fields. As you resonate with the tachyon pulse, your rate of vibration increases. Then, in meditation, you will be able to duplicate that higher vibration by yourself. The goal is to use tachyon energy to help you access deeper states of consciousness. Eventually, you will be able to access these states without tachyon stones.

The sources of tachyon energy are actually outside your solar system. The energy is coming in through cosmic forces, through comets, and so forth. Tachyon refers to the star of the same name, which is known to many galactic travelers. The source of this energy is believed to originate from that star system. The information about tachyon energy and the technology for its use are extremely important and useful for you now. You will need to learn several methods, including the tachyon method, for accelerating your processes.

What we are saying now is very important: All of you will find it necessary to accelerate your energy fields. When you are not accelerating, when you are physically or mentally stuck in some way, that is a sign that you need to have an acceleration. Do not be afraid to accelerate. What might be most useful is to accelerate your connections as well—that is, accelerate your contacts with your guides and extraterrestrial beings. Simply put, many of you will get stuck in lower energy patterns. It will be very difficult to get out without assistance, so do not hesitate to use the contacts you have with us.

SOUND AND COLOR

The sound of the name tachyon is very powerful. You can increase the power of the tachyon energy by speaking the word itself, which will help release the power of the stones. Tachyon is a galactic word, similar to the Hebrew word *Zohar*, or "the brilliance."

Sound enhances tachyon healing. It is useful to play certain music during healings, including computer-generated sounds. The music helps both the healer and the receiver to resonate with the pulse. Once you both are in resonance with the tachyon pulse, then powerful healing can take effect. It can be described as a settling in. In order to get the full benefit of the tachyon treatment, you must be open to it, and resonate with the pulse.

There are various levels of sound vibrations that can be used to accelerate the healing. For example, using a slow rhythmic sound will help you to enter a trance state. As you become more comfortable, the speed of the rhythms can be increased. The receiver's vibration will increase as the rhythm of sounds increases in speed. To give you an idea of the effects of sound, we will help the channel reproduce useful sounds when doing a tachyon treatment. [Chants:] *Tac . . . tac . . .* Various levels and speeds of sound vibrations can be used. For example, using that sound slowly will help the person you are healing slow his or her pulse. First, have the person adjust to the energy field by listening to a slow-paced sound. Then you can raise the speed of the sound to help the person increase his or her vibration. Tachyon energies used this way will raise the person's overall vibration, which will be very healing.

We want to speak briefly about the use of color with tachyon energy. Colors that can be especially useful are in the range of the magentas, the reds, the blues, and the purples. The effects of tachyon energy can be accelerated by the proper use of colors. We recommend that when you work with people seeking tachyon treatment, you set up a room with special lights. Also, be sensitive to the colors in the room.

For example, it would be helpful to use a special sheet or blanket of the colors mentioned above. The colors that the healer wears can be important, too, as part of the integrative approach of a tachyon energy treatment. The more you are aware of harmonizing all environmental aspects, the more powerful the tachyon treatment will be.

Tachyon energy can be used to enhance meditation. The stones can accelerate thought patterns of universal healing through the life force energy. An actual cellular reawakening can occur after a tachyon treatment. Tachyon energy can also affect eyesight in a positive way. Corrective work can be done with tachyon stones, especially when done in conjunction with color therapy.

TACHYON HEALING SESSIONS

Tachyon items, when placed around your body, help you to resonate with the pulsation and harmonious flow of the stones. Tachyon healing works by helping you to resonate with the stone's pulsation. Your vibratory fields and your auric fields will be enhanced. The acceleration from the tachyon energy, however, can be overpowering. That is why we want you to be careful to monitor it.

In the beginning, we recommend short periods of treatment so that the person can build up to the tachyon energy. A beginning treatment may be twelve to fourteen minutes long, combined with a polarity balancing, alignment, or gentle massage afterward. As you work with a person over a period of time, he or she may be able to tolerate twenty-eight minutes. Treatment time goes up in sevens. Thus, you can go from fourteen to twenty one to twenty-eight minutes. It is important to stick to the factor of seven in determining the length of the treatments. We do not recommend that you go beyond the twenty-eight minute limit unless there is a specific purpose for lengthening the treatment. Most will find twenty-eight minutes more than sufficient.

We recommend as well a twenty-eight minute balance afterward. If you work with someone for fourteen minutes of tachyon treatment, then we recommend a fourteen minute period afterward for energy balancing using non-touching techniques. Do not physically touch the person until after the fourteen-minute balance period. The reason for this is that the person's energy field is still in a state of flux. The energy is still sensitive, and you must respect this sensitivity. We recommend that the person receiving the treatment continue to follow his own pulse in meditation after the tachyon stones are removed. This will help to continue the healing effects and will enhance the balancing.

To stimulate just one area without an overall balancing can be productive, but it will not have as long-lasting an effect as using an integrated approach. It is better to have a treatment with the stones in which there is balancing and an integration of the energy. That insures that the whole system is put into balance. If you have a problem and treat that area alone, the original unbalance that manifested could switch to another area later. We prefer that the tachyon work be done by a healer who can use a more integrative approach. When the healer works with the person in an integrated way, then effective treatment can occur by leaving the tachyon energy near the body for longer periods. If the healer uses the tachyon energy alone, without a corresponding balancing, then longer tachyon healing will not be as beneficial.

The body should not get too used to tachyon energy. Because it is such a powerful energy, it is important to maintain the body's sensitivity to it. Compare the tachyon treatment to a drug that is used daily. A drug tolerance is easily built up, and then it is not as effective. The dosage has to be increased in order to obtain the same effect. Similarly, a tolerance can be built to the tachyon treatments as well. It is best to balance the usage of it, using it in separate periods with mental balancing, concentrated awareness of the pulsations, and an attempt to integrate and harmonize with the energy.

BUILDING AN ENERGY COCOON

Humans, as galactic beings, are highly intelligent beings. We know that you do not believe how intelligent you are because of the many emotional problems that are on the planet, and the many emotional problems that you have all experienced personally. This is not a criticism, but simply an observation. Your emotional bodies on the Earth are very underdeveloped. We wonder at times how you are able to keep yourself in balance at all, because your emotional bodies are constantly being submitted to the deviant electromagnetic energy that is bombarding your planet from man-made sources.

It is the deviant electromagnetic radiation that is coming from your nuclear bombs that are being tested, the deviant electromagnetic energy coming from the high-frequency and low-frequency radio sources that are being experimented with by your government, and deviant electromagnetic waves created by so many of the airplanes that are flying overhead. We could go on and on. Fortunately, you are such resilient beings. For the most part, you are able to adapt. But it would be highly beneficial to create a cocoon of energy around yourselves for your own protection.

The cocoon of energy will provide stability around your electromagnetic fields. Your cocoon energy needs to be strengthened so that you will not experience auric fractures. This is what is happening now. When auric fractures occur, you can experience deviant electromagnetic energies that can create discomfort.

You have heard that an energy cocoon can also be called a protective bubble of white light. What is important is that this white light, or cocoon, be sensitive enough to block electromagnetic radiation and some of the other energy sources that you do not want to experience. Auric fractures can occur from distorted electromagnetic energy. These fractures can trigger what you have called the déjà vu experience.

We will give you instructions on how to create this cocoon around you, because it is going to be vital for all of you to learn how to protect yourselves. You need to do this for many reasons. The most prominent reason is that you must keep your mental balance. We could not travel through the many different zones that we do, or travel within the galactic sphere unless we were able to control ourselves mentally, and control our fields of energy.

Most extraterrestrial beings will not come into physical manifestation because they do not want to expose themselves to the lower electromagnetic vibrations. This is going to be one of the biggest problems in your culture when you finally realize the dangers that you are exposing yourselves and your children to from distorted electromagnetic vibrations. It is everywhere on the planet now, and to come onto this planet and into this manifestation requires high levels of protection from the cocoon.

To create the cocoon, we ask that you start with a star tetrahedron (Star of David) approximately three to four feet above your head. From that star, bring twelve lines down in a sloping fashion, continuing until they reach below your body around your feet. You must do that for each vertical line. Then make a cross line that will move horizontally around your body so

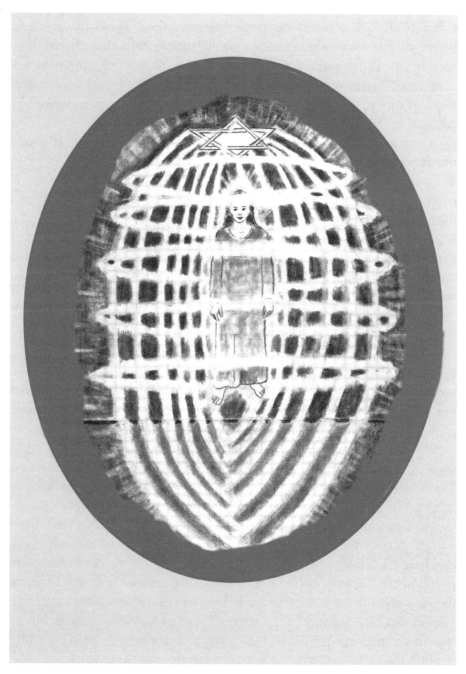

The Energy Cocoon

Gudrun Miller

that you now have ninety-degree intersecting lines. Build five of those horizontal lines on one side and five on the another side, each crisscrossing each other. At that point you will have twelve intersecting grid lines (see diagram). This is very important that you have established twelve grid lines. Then you will be able to access our own energy field as well as be centered in the energy field that you have created.

Once you are in the energy field you have just created, you can sound our expression. [Makes a fast, repeating sound:] *Tac . . . tac. . . tac . . .* This sound will clear out all extraneous electromagnetic energy that is coming to you. Now put a layer of white light around your cocoon, and then a then a layer of blue light, and finish with a layer of silver light. Now your cocoon is complete. We hope you have been trying to do this as you read these words. You will now be in a state of protection, and you can bring yourself into a state of balance where you have harmonized and stabilized your own electromagnetic vibrations.

BRINGING BACK GALACTIC IMAGES

For those who have built their cocoons, you can be beamed up into an area on our ships in a dimensional holding pattern. You can come into our ships and you will rest peacefully. You can move into a special room we have for you, a room of silver-blue healing light. Your intellectual capabilities are manifested through the brain. The spirit force that guides your brain is an electromagnetic vibrational energy. You will be cleansed and sharpened as this silver-blue light comes into that part of your soul that manifests your mental intelligence.

Still on our ship, we will spin the whole room that you are in in a tight fast circle and heightened centrifugal force. Feel the room continue to circle, continue to increase in vibration, continue to go round faster, faster and faster. Look out of the room that we are in on the ship and see the stars that are before you, the stars of the Arcturian system. Feel the starlight from those blue stars that you can see. Know that for some, this is your home system, and we have been patiently waiting for you to return. Do not worry about the time frame, because we are not in Earth time. It is not a problem of patience as you may think of it from your linear perspective.

See the stars and the Arcturian stargate, and see the image of those coming into the stargate that is protected by the Arcturians. As these higher consciousness beings enter the stargate from one side, they leave going through the stargate, leaving in pure spirit, in pure galactic form. It is a spiritual graduation. As you are beginning to access our energy, we ask you to bring some of these galactic images that you have back into reality so that others can see them. Sharing these images will activate others to remember their source.

This is such an important exercise because so many of you are struggling with your self-image. It has been shattered by so many forces impacting your emotional body and severely distorted by the negative implants that are constantly coming to you. The goal, however, is not to completely remember who you are, because it will throw you off balance if you have not fully accomplished the clearing process. Focus on clarity, on the stability of the mental process, and the remembering will occur. Some will remember differently than others. That is because some have a different perspective. Do not be confused by those having different memories. Go with your own soul memory.

Gently rock yourselves around, and spin yourselves down from our ship into a place where you can re-enter your own consciousness in your physical body. Spin yourself down, your bodies are happy to receive your spirits. Your mind has been charged, cleansed, cleared, and activated.

CHAPTER 9

OPENING YOUR CONSCIOUSNESS

You are living in a culture and a dimension that is quite restrictive to your consciousness, which you are wanting to expand as wide as possible. The expansion of your consciousness is the only requirement that will enable you to go into the next dimension. You are not required to be in any certain physical condition, but your consciousness and your awareness must be expanded. Seeking the help of the Arcturians can assist you in achieving the expansion of your consciousness, as well as amplifying and transforming yourself.

We have talked to you about expanding your consciousness through unlocking codes. The words "Holy, Holy, Holy is the Lord of Hosts" have traditionally been a code that can be used to expand your consciousness. Some of you, however, do not relate to Biblical phrases. Just as Jesus uses the name Sananda, there are new codes, new words, and new concepts that can be more appropriately used to open up your consciousness. We will work with you to help you direct your energies, but you alone must generate the openings.

You can better understand denseness when you obtain a higher perspective. This sounds simple. You have already experienced the dense energy that is surrounding the planet. There is a slowness and a fog-like quality that surrounds many third-dimensional activities. If you open your consciousness, you can rise above this dimension, and you will clearly comprehend the thickness of this space.

We also acknowledge the importance of the protection of your personal energy fields. Stray energies may enter when you open your consciousness wider. Many of you, in previous lifetimes, have had some misfortunes concerning people who were not open, or did not have sacred regard for this opening of the consciousness. It is a sacred task, a holy task. We are providing protective energy around all of you, as you are engaging in the process of opening your consciousness wider. With practice, it will become very easy to leave your body and move your consciousness higher.

CHANNELING

Channeling is one of many avenues that we now use to reach out to starseeds who are eagerly interested in connecting with us. Understand that you are responding to a primordial response from your brothers and sisters in the galaxy. All on your planet have the inherent capabilities to communicate with those in other parts of the galaxy. This is part of the genetic structure of your species.

We are coming through the channel as a group entity. This is what you would call a group-process channel, and several Arcturian ships assigned to this sector of the solar system are working with the channel on this project. It is extremely important that all of you learn to interface with the Arcturians and other extraterrestrials of a spiritual nature. It is time that you open up your consciousness to other cosmic influences. You will need this different perspective that we can offer.

Many different factors are involved in the channeling process. The term channeling is somewhat misleading, because what the channel is really doing is telepathically communicating with us. Through this telepathic communication, the channel is reporting what messages he is receiving from us. The personality of the channel does color the information that is brought forth. The receiving personality will inevitably influence and color some of the information that comes through.

Each channel will bring down whatever they can to the best of their ability. There is no channel now who will be 100 percent accurate in the total transferring of thought patterns. The only entity who was able to do that was Sananda-Jesus, and he was able to bring down 100 percent pure light. Others, such as your religious leaders, have brought down a strong light. But there was always some step down in the vibration, allowing for distortion of the information. It is natural for this to occur.

So when you are listening to channels, please use discernment, and allow for the fact that there may be some non-intentional distortion in the information that any channel will bring down.

Some of you have spoken about mathematic symbols and equations coming into your minds while you are in meditation, dreaming, or even when you just close your eyes for a moment. This is a sign that you are open to a telepathic power. We wish to communicate mathematically with many beings. Mathematics is a universal language with universal symbols throughout the galaxy. Even though you may not understand the equations now, rest assured that these equations are a form of symbolism that will help people understand the nature of cosmic reality.

Negative energies and entities can also be channeled. Deception has been used in channeling as a way of control or manipulation. A mistrust of this energy that you call channeling is ingrained in the human consciousness of many people. This comes from some of the earlier periods on the Earth when people were manipulated by false prophets and false religious leaders. This does not mean that channeling is bad or that it does not provide a practical way of communicating. Let us be clear that there is a great need to communicate with you now. Many restrictions keep us from appearing directly in your dimension. The telepathic form of communication is the most desirable now. Channeling can be very helpful, but it can also be misused or misguided. Do not rely totally on securing all your information from channels. Rely also on direct experiences and direct communications. Spend more time with your ascended masters and guides rather than focusing too much time on other human channels.

We wish for you to receive light, knowledge, and information, for you are opening your chakras. We are working with you to enhance your telepathic powers. You should view spiritual groups as a powerful training ground for telepathic work. Like-minded people need to come together in groups. This is important in telepathic communications; that is, you have a resonance with the like-mindedness of others. You are like-minded with us also. This like-mindedness has to do with a spiritual energy and a commitment to spiritual development. This is our highest commitment.

WALK-INS

The question of walk-ins is a very relevant one in these times, when many are questioning their missions on the planet. The issue of walk-ins is filled with confusion, myth, and misrepresentation, and the very term "walk-in" seems to be confusing. We prefer to use the term "spiritual visitor." It sounds like one spirit suddenly leaves and another entity comes in instantaneously. Although there have been cases like that, most of the walk-ins enter gradually. The process proceeds with continual communication between the higher self of the Earth person and the soul of that entity wishing to enter third-dimensional existence. It is not always true that the host soul leaves the body for the walk-in. There can be joint residency. Just as you have more than two people living in a house, there can be several spirits inhabiting a body.

The cooperation of a higher spirit from another dimension can greatly enhance the lives of those on the Earth plane. In most cases, those who have spiritual visitors from another dimension have been in life positions in which they have felt stuck. They were failing, and unable to progress in their life patterns. When it appears that nothing is to be gained by continuing the incarnation, then it is totally permissible, even advantageous, for a higher spirit to join and help activate the host person. This is a growth experience for the host spirit, and it is a chance for the higher-dimensional spirit to direct the host toward his or her mission or purpose. The highest mission the walk-in can perform is to ensure that a human being follows his or her path.

Let us look briefly at the seeding of your planet. It is well known by many that your planet was seeded by entities from outside your solar system. Many are still struggling with the ideas of evolution and other primitive concepts that have been explained in your mythology, but a seeding did take place. The walk-in phenomenon began with the seeding of your planet. It was impossible for such a leap of consciousness and evolution of human life to occur without assistance from those in higher places. The final evolutionary step was completed when a spirit came into physical manifestation. Bringing in other entities began with the first prototype of your human form, when the first series of human beings were developed. The evolutionary chain was manipulated. If you think that walk-ins are an unusual phenomenon, think again.

These are difficult concepts to understand. A leap of faith is often necessary in order to comprehend that interdimensional existence is truly a reality, and that extraterrestrials have come to your planet to communicate with you.

The Mission of Walk-ins

Why, you ask, would an entity want to come to this planet now, when many of you are waiting so eagerly to leave? So much density, destruction, and violence exists on the planet. You often feel that you are in a fog. Why would anyone actually choose to come here? Generally, unless you are in the Earth's incarnational cycle, there is no need to return to physical manifestation. Only those who have a particular mission or a particular goal in mind would really want to come here. The mission of those who are walking in relates mainly to anchoring energy and receiving and activating high vibrations, although each walk-in is in a slightly different situation.

Walk-ins are working on consciously receiving the light and the thought patterns of those who are beyond your dimensional space. The more people who can receive information and thought waves from those beyond the planet, the more this planet will be activated. More of you will then be ready to move your awareness into a higher dimension. In order to start the chain, it is necessary to have more and more people who are sensitive to the higher energies. It is like the hundredth-monkey phenomenon; it is a chain reaction.

Walk-ins can help establish a reawakening, anchoring, activation, and awareness of galactic forces. Group consciousness can then be activated on the planet. This would be an acceptable description for those who are seeking to understand their roles. Some walk-ins are searching for a specific task, but they should not conceive of their missions as entailing specific jobs, that is, a third-dimensional linear process. Those who are struggling with the walk-in phenomenon might get stuck because they cannot find a particular job, such as when your famous Noah built an ark for survival. Specific tasks will emerge.

Meanwhile, the transformations that are really going to be meaningful will focus on awareness, communication, and consciousness. These are the three main forces that are shaping those who are moving toward an expanded transformation. Of the three, at this time, the most important is communication. It is important that you talk with others about what you are receiving. You will then activate their abilities to transmute into a higher dimension.

SPIRITUAL COHABITATION

Cohabiting with a higher being serves as a way of allowing you to access other planes of awareness. This function illustrates one way in which walk-ins help those with whom they are in cohabitation. Cohabitation activates the host and generates an improvement. There should be a lighter quality and a higher energy level, resulting in more of a sense of ease about the person. If you are not sensing that about the host, then something is wrong. Cohabitation with a walk-in is definitely a heightened phenomenon that is done with conscious acceptance of the host's higher self. It is not done against his or her will. A higher spiritual energy will work with a person only after an invitation from that person's higher self.

If, at any time, that person does not want that entity to be present, then the spirit is gone. It is that simple. The fact is, when you connect with such an energy, you want it around more. Imagine, if you will, that you are looking for your etheric double, or your soul mate. Suddenly, you have contact with that soul mate. It is a phenomenon that many of you might even have experienced in your dreams, and then felt disappointed when the dream was over because you had lost the connection. Unlike dreams, you maintain that contact in the walk-in phenomenon. This is the type of strong connection you have during the walk-in phenomenon. You feel excited to have such a connection.

The purpose of cohabitation is to provide an expansion of spiritual awareness for the Earthly host. Cohabitation ends any time the host wants it to end, but there does not need to be an end. The end (remember, we are talking about your linear perspective) can occur when the mission has been accomplished. Let us say, for example, that you are in a classroom taking a course from an instructor who is teaching you basic mathematics lessons. That teacher will stay with you throughout the semester, but when you graduate and move on, you will not need that instructor any more. So it is with cohabitation. Spirit walk-ins are serving as guides or instructors. The walk-in experience can end when the specific need has been fulfilled. You may then release the entity, or you may choose to stay in contact.

In terms of cohabitation, think about the life of Sananda-Jesus. Jesus, while in physical incarnation, was able to link up with the highest Christ energy. There is a high spiritual energy that you refer to as the Son of Man energy. This energy was able to co-inhabit the body of the man you know as Jesus, creating a powerful and beneficial experience for humankind.

THE MERGING PROCESS

The physical body can struggle in the beginning of a walk-in experience. Sometimes there is no meld, no true harmony. That is because the walk-in that enters is coming from a higher plane than the host. That can cause some disruptions in the host's overall awareness, and those kinks might be perceived in his or her body, since the body reflects the spiritual blocks and disharmony caused by negative thinking. You might find that your bodies want to do unusual things, such as making particular movements or uttering strange sounds. This is happening in order to release blocked energy. The blocks remain when you cannot successfully release the energy that builds up, and then the body will break down.

Many of you might say that this walk-in experience sounds crazy. You might say that there is a schizophrenic aspect to it. But remember, this is a heightened energy we are talking about, not an energy of distortion. The host of a walk-in becomes more himself instead of less so. He becomes more confident, for it enhances who he already is. If you are feeling confused about walk-ins, you are probably thinking that people must give up their original self to accommodate a walk-in. This is where the confusion lies. The self is not given up; it is enhanced. If you see people who claim to be walk-ins but are more dense than they were before, then you know they are thinking incorrectly.

People can experience the walk-in phenomenon and not be conscious of it. On a conscious level, they can be unaware of it, but on a higher level, it has been agreed upon. On the lower level, it can be experienced as a gradual awakening. When it is brought to the consciousness of the host, there must be an acceptance of the walk-in state, or else the experience will terminate. Once there is awareness, continual communication can take place between the walk-in entity and the host.

Walk-in communication is much like a higher form of channeling. A walk-in can live with a person throughout the day and help that person in their daily affairs. It is one way for an extraterrestrial entity to introduce himself, for a gradual introduction is preferable to a sudden appearance. The walk-in spirit does not have to be present twenty-four hours a day. It is almost always more of a coexistence rather than a total takeover. In most cases in which there has been a total takeover, it has been planned well in advance. In actuality, a total takeover is very dangerous, unless certain guidelines and restrictions are followed.

Thousands of Arcturians are currently functioning as walk-ins on the Earth plane. They cohabit with Earthly hosts and stay in direct communication with us. There are also walk-ins from other planetary sources. Some have caused problems because they have violated the basic rules of this phenomenon. Unfortunately, those who have weaker senses of self and weaker personalities can become confused by negative entities. Remember that the entity must always leave when there is a firm rejection by the soul of the human.

NEGATIVE COHABITATION

Be forewarned, however: You must use discrimination, for there are examples in your culture of negative cohabitation. People who are engaged in violence and acting crazy sometimes pretend that they are being possessed. They talk themselves into thinking others are forcing them to perform negative acts. It is a delusion. It is simply their own lower self, very primitive energies that have been activated within them. What you will see is a lowering of energy as the more primitive mechanisms are being activated.

There have been cases in which people have wrongly believed that they were inhabited by a spirit. Initially, they were partly inhabited but then they allowed their ego to get involved. When a person wants to use the walk-in experience for selfgratification on the physical plane, that energy can become greatly distorted. They could have very negative experiences. It is true that there are dark forces in the universe. It is true that there are negative extraterrestrials who are interested in human domination.

You have had men such as Hitler who have brought down negative collective energy. He was not acting alone. He was able to activate other negative forces that were seeking control. He was able to call in these energies and transform himself in a negative way.

Know that you can use thought rejection, which involves renouncing negative attachments to what some of you call evil. You can protect yourself, so that negativity does not stick to your auric fields. You will be impervious to negative energies, so your spirit will be able to move through the clouded etheric energy field of the Earth without harm. You will find that there are many places where you can get stuck in the density and darkness, many energies that could attach themselves to you. You do not want this. You can prevent this sticking by using thought rejection.

Since there is confusion and much stuckness in the energies around the planet, you generally need as much spiritual assistance as you can find. As you rise above these low densities, you might welcome the assistance that can be offered by a walk-in. Let us focus on the heightened use of the walk-in energy. Sananda and the core workers of his Brotherhood/Sisterhood are continually making contact, encouraging people to open up on a spiritual basis. The walk-in phenomenon will continue to increase, because there is a need for an energy infusion in order for humanity and the Earth to take the next evolutionary step. Right now, the planet is mired in negativity, and it is in great danger. Assistance will be given in any way possible.

CHAPTER 10

DIMENSIONS AND CORRIDORS

We are interested in how you as a species will accept the knowledge of the higher dimensions. This represents a major evolutionary step in your development. Earlier in the planet's history, there was a very limited understanding of dimensions. Dimensional awareness has emerged only during the past five thousand years. The development of religion usually indicates that a species is becoming aware of other dimensions. The first step in dimensional awareness focuses on the development of a religion, and an understanding of the existence of a greater being. The concept of a heaven is a prime example of elementary dimensional awareness.

We study the dimensions from different parts of the galaxy. Various places in the galaxy offer different entry points into other dimensions. If you could actually see how one dimension layers on top of another, you would see that there is a bulge when life exists in a particular solar system or on a planet. This bulge is very thick. It becomes the texture for the karmic fields that are developing on the planet.

Planets can coexist in different dimensions. Karmic developments also leave traces in other dimensions. Karma is the dense energy that can be seen when we come into the dimensional area of the Earth. Although it is a dense energy, it is a fantastically interesting energy and we can easily read it. The information exists in the bulge—the karmic areas that exist layer upon layer around your planet. It is easy for the

Arcturians, the Pleiadians, and other advanced civilizations to read this energy and see into your past.

Some extraterrestrials have visited your planet and manifested themselves, which has caused some disruptions. They have not understood the transformations that can occur because of their manifestations, nor the effects on themselves of being in this unique dimensional arena that has developed on the Earth plane. Imagine going underwater. Even if you have studied the underwater geography, you still do not totally understand its effects.

Some of the higher-dimensional entities who have come to the planet have not needed to manifest. They are sophisticated enough to be able to gather any necessary information without manifesting. There is key information on this planet that would be of use to others— information that could relate to the development of the whole galaxy, to the Creator energy, and to the particular angle of dimension that is uniquely available from the Earth. Many want to study how this planet becomes aware of the transformation into multidimensional existence.

We are happy that many of you are grasping the significance of multidimensional existence, because it is the key to ascension and the key to a higher evolutionary phase. When you acknowledge the existence of other dimensions, then you can access them. Acknowledge that we, the Arcturians and others, are existing in other dimensions. Acknowledge our existence and that we interact with you to help you in your enlightenment. One overriding message of the ascension is that other dimensions do exist and that you have a way to access them.

THE FOURTH DIMENSION

We realize that there might be some confusion about the fourth dimension. The fourth dimension is tied in with the Earth's incarnational cycle. It is the Earth's sense of a physical body, or the sense of time and places, as you know them. These places, however, are now expanded. They do not fit into the third-dimensional framework, but they are connected to its existence. The fifth dimension is free of the Earth as the reference point. In the fifth dimension, you have a spirit body that can assume forms that are unknown to you now.

In the fourth dimension, you will assume a form similar to your current physical body. In the fifth dimension, you can assume forms that you have never seen before or even imagined from your third-dimensional framework. Many of your conceptions of heaven, for example, and where you are going in your evolution, are more focused in the fourth dimension. The fourth dimension is also more closely tied to the astral plane.

The fourth dimension is a wonderful place to be. It is a natural progression. Why, then, would you desire to leap past the fourth into the fifth dimension? You have been in the fourth dimension before. It is not a new place for you. Some people may tell you that by skipping the fourth dimension, you are going to miss a huge aspect that you cannot make up. We are telling you that you have been in the fourth dimension before through parts of your Earth incarnations, and in between those incarnations.

People speak of the fourth dimension all of the time when they are talking to you about their near-death experiences. They might refer to going down the long white tunnel, and then meeting friends and relatives. Many people on the Earth who have passed on are still residing on the fourth dimension.

Many people on the fourth dimension will be able to ascend into the fifth dimension when the ascension occurs. What about those who die before the ascension? Will those people be able to ascend as well? The answer is yes; there will be an ascension from the fourth dimension. If you die for some reason before the ascension, then you will go to the fourth dimension and wait. There are ascension groups in the fourth dimension. We are also working with groups of forty in that dimension. If you were to go to the fourth dimension, you would feel very comfortable. You all enter that dimension frequently in your sleep, and the animal spirits reside in the fourth dimension as well.

THE FIFTH DIMENSION

The fifth dimension is a dimension of light, of restfulness, and of total mental openness—openness to the thoughts of others. There is no need to hide any thinking. Thoughts are immediately transmitted by directing them to a person. If you do not wish your thoughts to be heard, then simply think them without direction. This is a very important message that we have for you about telepathy. When you do want to transmit a message, then contact the other person mentally. It is a misconception that when you communicate through telepathy, all thoughts are open to everyone. An inherent code of respect is in place. We receive only those messages that are meant to be transmitted to us. We will not invade your privacy. At the same time, we will acknowledge what you want to transmit to us.

Coming into the fifth dimension will give you the opportunity to be with your galactic friends. To come to the fifth dimension, however, is going to require a higher frequency, a higher sharpness, and a higher intensity. This is why we have the stargate—to insure that you refine your energy, and bring yourself to that frequency which would allow you to exist in the fifth. Those in the fifth dimension can easily move through the fourth dimension. It is not like going from the fifth to the third, which does require a certain amount of skill. From the fifth to the fourth is as easy as falling asleep and going into a dream state.

Moving from the fifth to the third dimension does require that one has achieved an ascendancy and masterhood. It does require a special guidance and overviewing. We are not guardians of that process. The guardians of the process of moving from the fifth dimension to third dimension are under the realms of Sananda and Kuthumi.

We know you want to come into the realm of our mother ships and travel interdimensionally. How can you do that? When you raise your consciousness, you can create beautiful thought projections, and you can move your spirit into the higher realms. You can project yourselves through a tunnel of light, through a hole in the space you call the third dimension. It is not really a hole as you know it, but an opening or a corridor that you can enter with your consciousness. Imagine that this opening exists in your mind. Bring your consciousness to the opening, and go into this corridor of light with us now. Go through the tunnel of light—you can hear a whistling sound . . . come into our fifth dimension.

The dimensions themselves are layered on top of each other. When you are in the fifth dimension of our home planet, even though that dimension is not visible to the Earth, it is still within the fifth-dimensional realm of the galaxy, and occupies fifth-dimensional space in the Arcturus system. The Earth has not yet manifested its fifth-dimensional vibration. As we are working to help you to bring your own vibration up into the fifth dimension, we are simultaneously helping to bring the Earth into the fifth-dimensional realm as well. This is an important point to understand. The third-dimensional realm will still remain in a limited sense after the planetary ascension.

We are involved in helping to develop fifth-dimensional portals and fifth-dimensional grid lines for the Earth. We, as well as the Pleiadians, are very involved in this project. This huge cosmic project is going very well, and is nearly one half completed. We do not want it to be a jolt to the Earth, but it will be experienced in many ways as a shock when it happens. There are many on the third-dimensional side of the veil who are working to connect with higher energy and higher beings. By doing this, you are effectively helping us in the overlapping and interlocking of the two dimensions. This will be a most powerful transformation for you, and a delight for us. One of the great functions of the starseeds is to help with the interlocking process, the connecting of the third dimension with the fifth dimension.

FIFTH-DIMENSIONAL LIGHT

It is important that you understand how to interact with the fifth-dimensional light. Our grand mission, once again, centers solely on bridging the third dimension to the fifth. The Arcturians are able to send you specific light that can penetrate the third dimension, and thus arrive to you more easily. The energy transformation in the universe is set up on the basic pattern of a sender and a receiver. If energy is sent without a receiver, then the circuit is not completed. It is that simple. We are working with you to purify your ability to receive. When you allow yourself greater sensitivity, then you can pick up this fifth-dimensional energy.

The fifth-dimensional energy is continually being sent to you now in different forms. Some of this energy is being sent in the form of thought waves. There are those, like the channel, who are able to receive our thoughts. Other starseeds are receiving the fifth-dimensional energy as music. Some of them can even translate the Arcturian energy into beautiful music. A number of you can receive the Arcturian energy to create cosmic paintings and images. Some can receive the energy specifically through sounds and tones. A few gifted lightworkers can transmit this fifth-dimensional energy through their hands as healing energy. Any of you have the capability to bring healing, fifth-dimensional energy through your hands.

There are many ways in which this connection to the fifth dimension occurs. The connection to the fifth dimension can occur strongly during dreams. This connection may also occur through thought projection. With thought projection, you are seeking to place or project yourself into our arena, which includes our ships, our temples, and our home planet. You can actually move yourself into this arena. It is important now to amplify any means you have to access this fifth-dimensional light.

CORRIDORS

Corridors are connections between the third and fifth dimension, where a person who is in the third dimension can experience aspects, powers, and information from the fifth. The corridors are your connections to the fifth dimension. It is a verification, a living proof, and an experiential dimensional experience available to you now.

Using your current scientific terminology, a corridor is similar to a wormhole. It is a place where you enter, and then can go into another part of the universe directly instead of having to travel, say, one thousand light years. You can actually go into a wormhole and come out in another area without having to expend the linear time or the energy. The concept is the same for a corridor. You can enter a corridor, and you can go to the places that you would not normally be able to. This means that, for example, a corridor can bring you to a place in the fifth dimension.

We call them corridors, because it is like a vestibule in that you do not actually enter the realm, but you are close enough to experience and sense the energy of the realm. From your perspective, it brings you to a higher energy point. It also enables us to reach you in these places. For us to come down and interact with you requires a lowering of our vibrational field. We are not saying it is a lowering of our spiritual field, but it is a lowering of the physical vibrational field. When we meet you in the corridors, we do not have to step down our vibration but a slight degree. We have found in our work with you that you want to be raised to a higher vibration, or you would not be listening to us or working with us now. It is more desirable for you to come to a place where you have raised your vibration. You can then interact with us while you are in a heightened vibrational state.

The existence of the corridors is also related to the Photon Belt. You have read that the Photon Belt will not occur until sometime in the future, but, in reality, trails of photon energy have already reached the Earth. You think in linear time, thus you expect the Earth and the sun will enter the photon belt in a fixed year, such as the year 2000 or 2012. However, trails of introductory photon energy have already come into the Earth system. It is these trails that allow the creation and use of the corridors. The entry and exit ways of the corridors are to be used by you.

Corridors are projected down to the Earth by us and other high-energy beings. Corridors can be created to relate to specific frequencies or groups of people. The Arcturian corridors are set up for us to specifically interact with you, the starseeds. The corridors in which we work with you are very energetic. We can connect you through these corridors to our ships and to specific places on Arcturus. We can also direct specific corridors to places personally for you.

NATURALLY OCCURRING CORRIDORS

Corridors also occur naturally in the third dimension. The Egyptian pyramids, for example, were built on a natural corridor. They were carefully aligned with the star systems in the Orion constellation. Places on the Earth that have naturally occurring corridors are very useful and important. It is well advised for you to experience the energy at these particular corridors. The energy at these corridors is very general; thus you can direct yourself to many different places from these points. The specific corridors with which we have been working with you are mostly connected to our ports, and to fifth-dimensional Arcturian energy.

Natural corridors exist at power spots, which you also call vortexes. A large, multifaceted corridor can be found at the Montezuma Well near Sedona, Arizona. It is like a shopping mall, and you have a selection of many stores that are all together in one location. Many different corridors can be accessed from that point. Another powerful corridor complex is located in the area of Crestone, Colorado. This is a central energy point for us. We have made deep contacts within the mountains of that area, and we are able to use this point for transmitting and processing energy. It is a way station, you might say. Deep within the Earth, at that point, are very powerful crystals that assist us in transmitting energy to you. We can beam out energy to you, and we can beam out energy through the systems interacting with the corridors at this place called Crestone.

Corridors also exist along the electromagnetic grid lines of the Earth. The grid-line corridors are becoming more important as the Earth is attempting to shift into the fifth dimension. It is useful to do work within these corridors. The Native American Indians especially have been able to do such work. Many lightworkers are now traveling around the world opening up different corridors, and this has been very helpful. Please note that these corridors have been sometimes referred to as stargates, but they are, in reality, corridors. The significance of these corridors is being recognized, and activating them is very important. Many of these corridors have been closed for long periods of time due to the densities around the planet.

Corridors also connect the third and the fourth dimension. You actually enter into a corridor between the third and fourth dimension during the dream state, or when you are daydreaming. We, however, are working to move you into the higher realms of the fifth dimension.

CORRIDORS IN SPACE

Interdimensional corridors have also been created in outer space. If you wish to travel to another star system light years away, you can bring your spaceship into the Jupiter corridor. This is an actual corridor in your solar system that has been created by the Arcturians, the Pleiadians, and other higher beings. You can travel to that point called the Jupiter corridor, and proceed through the corridor to places many light years away. Your famous author Arthur C. Clarke, who is an Arcturian starseed, sensed the Jupiter corridor and described it in several of his books.

The Jupiter corridor is not the only corridor in or near your solar system. There is also a main corridor outside of your solar system. Corridors like this exist between star systems and, likewise, between different sectors of the galaxy. Corridors also exist between galaxies. Unfortunately, the existence of corridors cannot be validated by third-dimensional science. You cannot see the corridors with your telescopes, nor detect them with your current instruments.

ENTERING A CORRIDOR

An interdimensional corridor is an energy field; thus it can be seen or felt by those who are sensitive. Yes, there is a physical manifestation that can be viewed, but it requires a heightened awareness and sensitivity. We are helping you to develop that sensitivity. Those of you who are not highly trained may not experience the physicality of the corridors. However, the more you experience the energy within a corridor, your sensitivity to it will improve. You will raise your vibration by activating and accelerating your energies in the corridor. The corridor is an actual physical connection, but it is a connection on a higher frequency. Therefore, most people will not be able to see it.

All people have access to the corridors. However, to enter a corridor, you must have attained a certain frequency, a higher vibration in your energy field. Higher beings know that these corridors can provide a clear opportunity to communicate with you. It is much easier to reach us in the corridor. This is why we have always stated that it is better for you to come up to a higher dimensional level to see us and experience our energy, rather than for us to come down to your denser third-dimensional energy.

To enter a corridor, you should bring your physical body close to that area. Then you can initiate an out-of-body experience where your spirit and your etheric self leave your physical body, and go into the corridor. Many of you are traveling out ofbody while sleeping, and some of you who are highly skilled can travel out-of-body in regular meditations. In the out-of-body state, you can go into a corridor and travel to many different places.

To access the corridors, then, you must be at a higher frequency, and you must be able to leave your body. In the beginning, we recommend that you are as physically close to a corridor as possible. Later, you will be able to access the corridor remotely. We do want to tell you that safety valves exist in the corridor so that you cannot be trapped inside. There are currently safeguards that will prevent you from going into the fifth dimension. At the moment of ascension, however, you will be able to use the corridors, and very comfortably take your body with you up into the corridors. All of the entrances and passageways will be wide open for that period. In this manner, you can see that the corridors play a very significant role in the ascension process.

We want you to use the corridors, and lift yourself out of your body when you are confronting heavy densities. This is not an escape. This is simply a way for you to rise above the density. Know that there are now direct links from the Arcturian system to the planet Earth, and you can be a part of this system that establishes these links. With practice, you are going to be able to effectively activate the corridors at will.

INSIDE A CORRIDOR

There is a certain protective quality about a corridor. For example, if you were in an Earth-change catastrophe, you would find yourself protected in an interdimensional corridor. In the corridor, you can temporarily become invisible. You can waiver in frequency. By this, we mean that if someone saw you in the corridor and they were not in the corridor, then they would see you waiver or flicker.

Time does change inside the corridors. From the Earth perspective, you can experience a few hours passing by, but in the corridor it will seem like a very short time. The reverse is also true. A lot of this depends on what you need. It is important that your physical body be in a very safe place when you enter a corridor. You must be without hunger, but not overly full. The body must be in a good place to be relaxed.

While inside a corridor, you will be able to increase your awareness as you improve your electromagnetic vibrations and accelerate your energy levels and your thought processes. It is the boosting of your electromagnetic energy fields that is important. You have permission to work in the corridors. You can ask for our guidance, and we will be there, or you can go through them by yourself. You can also come to the Arcturian ships through the corridors.

There are higher extraterrestrials that are vibrating at such a high frequency, a frequency that is difficult for your physical form to be around, that contact with them would cause a distortion in your energy fields. Some of you would actually pass out if you were exposed to this kind of frequency. This is how high some of these beings are. But if you can raise your vibration, enter into a corridor, and meet a being such as this, the corridor would serve as a form of protection for you.

We bring down now a gray and silver-gray light form. This silver-gray is a bright silver ray and a shiny silver light. It is not like any light form that you have seen before. This silver-gray light form is a new beam that we offer you. Use it to cleanse yourself and awaken cellular knowledge, for the silver light is a light of protection in the corridors. When you go through a black hole, you might imagine that a disintegration of self and even a loss of consciousness will occur. The silver light that we are offering is a protection of consciousness and awareness. As you travel in a corridor with this silver light, there will be no loss of consciousness.

Know that your electromagnetic energy field is evolving just as your thought processes are. Now is the time to go into electromagnetic energy work. The silver-gray light is necessary to accelerate your vibrations. We bring the light down now because we know that you are ready for it. You are vibrating at a nice rate, but you can vibrate much higher than your current rate. There will be no problems for your body or your system to move to a higher frequency now. You can tolerate it, because your body is in balance to tolerate a higher frequency.

KEEPING THE CORRIDORS OPEN

We use the corridors to connect into your level of consciousness. But the spinning of the planet and the different levels of density continue to increase. The density itself is creating some difficulties. Third-dimensional energy is more and more difficult to see through. This is why it is important to keep these corridors open. This density is enveloping the planet on many levels. More people will find it more difficult to see through the reality of their existence. The density will be such that it will engender more hatred and darkness.

The issue is not how to close a corridor; it will close by itself. The issue is how to keep it open. If you are saying that you do not want someone to use a specific corridor, we would advise you not to worry about that. It could be compared to a person feeling nothing from the Sedona vortexes, which are huge natural corridors. Some people are not ready to vibrate at that higher frequency, but they may be affected if they stay around long enough. An open corridor cannot harm anyone. The kind of energy needed to close a corridor can be generated by various negative behaviors, such as consuming alcohol or drugs, watching violence on TV, fighting, screaming, swearing, or playing low-vibrational, negative music.

What we are saying is that we need to keep as many corridors open as possible. Corridors come in many varieties. The big ones are like the vortexes in Sedona or at Montezuma's Well in Arizona. Big corridors naturally exist in different parts of the country, and they need to be kept open. That is why groups will be meeting at certain places throughout the country to activate these corridors. This is a great spiritual service.

From our perspective in viewing the Earth process, we see the necessity for all starseeds to have a strong sense of detachment from the ongoing occurrences on the Earth. Conversely, you need to have a strong attachment to working in the corridors and integrating the energy vibrations coming to you from the higher realms. The corridors are becoming more and more important as the instability on the planet deepens. There is more pressure on the corridors, there is more need for the lightworkers to use them.

The corridors will become like a lifeline for you. We have set up corridors in many areas. There are power areas here in Arizona with the channel, and other areas are being developed in relation to the groups that form. Our goal with all the Group of Forty members is to establish at least 1,600 individual corridors around the world.

Perhaps each of you wish to develop other corridors around the area in which you live. By establishing new corridors, you are helping to solidify the dimensional interface, and helping to connect the third dimension with the fifth dimension. There is nothing more powerful that you can do now. We know that we could talk about cleaning the ocean, saving the forests, or clearing the air. While all of this is very important, each is but a small portion of the overall plan. When we look at the big picture, we see that the Earth needs more fifth-dimensional energy and higher vibrations, and it needs to release its dense, negative energy.

A Meeting in the Corridor

We are the Arcturians, and I am Juliano. Ask for the activation of a personal corridor above your head at this time. See a swirling corridor of energy open up above you now. Golden beams of light from one of our ships overhead is filling your corridor with bright light, and the corridor is expanded to encompass your entire living area. I will help to open this corridor wider, and help you to receive more of the energy in the corridor. I ask you to look into the corridor with your third eye, and you will see an image of me standing there.

I am surrounded by a golden halo as you look and see me. This halo is as much a protection for me as it is a sign of higher energy from your perspective. I am guided by this wonderful protective halo, for I am emerging from the fifth dimension into this corridor. The corridor is also of service to us when we are serving you. It serves us by providing a place for us to connect with you, since we do not yet want to appear in your third-dimensional realm.

Beam energy from your third eye outward as you are looking at the corridor. There is a huge ball of energy that I am now sending down. This ball of energy is made up of fifteen spheres combined into the shape of the Tree of Life. This tree actually has fifteen spheres instead of the ten spheres you see in your Jewish *Kaballah* Tree of Life. In our work, there are fifteen spheres. Receive the burst of energy from these fifteen spheres. The ball of light, the symbol of the fifteen spheres, is coming down and placing its energy into your third eye. It is your third eye that is activating the corridors. Feel the beams of light coming into your third eye as you are receiving this energy. This is Juliano.

CHAPTER 11

THE ARCTURIAN STARGATE

We approach the Arcturian stargate with deep reverence. It is a timeless experience there. The Arcturian stargate is a multidimensional gateway into the galaxy and beyond. The stargate is a central clearinghouse for galactic soul assignments. Imagine coming to a place where you enter one way, but on the other side you may have a hundred thousand different portals going to different areas in the galaxy. You will need assistance in aligning yourself to the right portal. Once you pass though a portal on the other side of the stargate, then you are committed to that process that you selected. For example, if you chose the portal to return to the Earth, then you will come into an Earth incarnation again. However, you may not want to do that. You may want to leave Earth permanently.

You can look at the stargate as an instructional, directive experience. Once you are in the stargate, we can help you look into each portal. You can see other existences that are possible for you to enter. You then have the ability to project your future in that possible existence. Based on that projection, you can then make a decision whether to enter that life. Some of you want to return to your home planets. You could still benefit more by spending time on Arcturus before returning to your home planet. Did you know that some of you came through the stargate before and chose the Earth portal? You came into this incarnation as starseeds. Some of you may decide to stay in the stargate system for a while. There are friends, soul mates if you will, that are waiting for you now in the stargate.

The stargate may be described as a multidimensional, holographic apparatus. It is not unidimensional, because it faces many different sides leading into different dimensions. It can be described as an infinitely large edifice that has many portals and many different healing centers. You may have come into the third-dimensional portal, but there also exists a fifth- and sixth-dimensional portal, as well as many portals to different areas in the galaxy.

The stargate is truly an interdimensional palace. Extended gardens and healing chambers, some of them multidimensional, can be found within this wonderful palace. The stargate houses many teachers who are there to work with you, to guide you, and to help you. We will work with you to bring you from the ascension into our ships, and from our ships to Arcturus and the stargate. It is exciting to imagine that many thousands of lightbodies from Earth will be coming to the stargate during the ascension.

The Arcturian stargate has been called the "jewel of the galaxy." Those who look upon the stargate directly are immediately transformed. It lives in the memories of your soul. Some of you have experienced the stargate as starseeds, and have come to the Earth through the stargate. In your meditations, you can now go to the area of the stargate. We can take you to chambers and vestibules around the stargate, but we cannot presently take you into it for processing. To be processed through it means that you have left the Earth, and you have left your body.

Not everyone on Earth will go through the stargate experience. Some of you are going to remain in certain incarnational groupings such as the Mormons or the Reverend Moon soul group. The stargate is only for starseeds, and those who have come into their awareness as galactic dimensional beings. Not all of you have come to that point in your evolution, and, frankly, some of you do not want to. You will find that there are other methods of evolution in the universe, but none as effective as the stargate. The Arcturian stargate is for evolving galactic citizens. The stargate activates higher dimensional existences. It connects to the sixth and seventh dimensions as well as the fifth. You cannot be shown those, however, until you have been purified.

Two other galactic stargates exist besides the Arcturian stargate, although they are not as developed as ours. Our galaxy has been divided into three major areas. The three stargates cover the three sectors of our Milky Way galaxy. The Arcturian stargate is connected to the other two stargates. We can send you from this stargate into the other stargates as well.

GUARDIANS OF THE STARGATE

The control and maintenance of the stargate is a very important function in this galaxy. Anyone who reaches a level that permits them to leave the Earth's incarnational cycle, and also wishes to go to higher planes or higher planets in other dimensions within our local system, will have to pass through the stargate.

The Arcturians are the guardians and the administrators of the stargate. We are currently responsible for the stargate, and thus it is referred to as the Arcturian stargate. Other beings are in training to help us. We are getting much assistance from the Pleiadians on this. We do have other species helping that are very evolved and that you are not familiar with.

We are close to the Earth, as you know. It is our closeness to this sector of the galaxy that brings us into a special relationship with you. But it is not the actual physical proximity as much as it is our spiritual achievements and our fifth-dimensional presence that brings us to you. It is also why the stargate is in our area. The stargate itself and the administration of the stargate is passed on every 52,000 years to another holder. If another holder is not ready, then it will stay with the Arcturians for an equivalent period of time. It is an honor to be the holders of the stargate for this wonderful process of planetary ascension that lies before you.

FUNCTIONALITY OF THE STARGATE

The Arcturian stargate is an individual spiritual manifestation like a planet, a star, or a black hole. The stargate is a creation, an energy force that is unique, and it has a development and an evolution of its own. Each person passing through the stargate temporarily becomes part of it, and you, in a sense, participate in the energy and the consciousness of the stargate.

The stargate is evolving to become a higher-dimensional doorway. It is evolving toward where it will become totally transformed into the next dimension. Then it will become a doorway from the fifth dimension into the sixth. The stargate can hold millions of souls. If you would describe it as a space, it would be hard to put a time-space coordinate on it, because being a gateway into the fifth dimension, it is considered part of the fifth dimension. In the fifth dimension, space and time have a different meaning. We cannot give you a physical sense of the stargate. We can only say that the stargate is as big as it needs to be.

The stargate is open only for a limited time. Some of you have actually been on a planet, even on the Earth, and you were not able to reincarnate into another galactic planetary system because the stargate was closed. Some souls were, by necessity, forced to stay on the Earth until the stargate reopened. Many of you who are starseeds will know the path to the stargate, and you will use it. It will be like a reawakening of memories. It will very comfortable for you.

Eventually, this stargate will be closed when the current tasks are completed. When the graduated souls complete their transition, the stargate will be closed. The stargate portals open and close at different times. We are at a period in an evolutionary pattern of this galactic section when the stargate is open to the Earth. It has a cycle, and the cycle opens and closes. You are in a period where you can participate in its opening. This is part of the reason why many of you have come to the Earth as starseeds, as people from other planets, because you knew that you could return and go back through the stargate again.

The stargate opens and closes to different sections of the galaxy. Your section is now open. This is hard to explain, because this is a multidimensional concept. For example, we can say that the stargate is closed, but that could mean that the stargate is closed only to the Earth. It opened to the Earth in 1987, and will be open at least until 2012, possibly to 2017. There will be periods after that when it will reopen, but this is the core time, or the optimal time. Understand that you must take advantage of this. By approaching the stargate, you can bypass the fourth-dimensional reincarnational cycle.

THE HEALING AND PURIFICATION PROCESS

The Arcturian stargate can be thought of as a healing chamber, a healing portal where we will assist you in your final purification for ascension. Specifically, the healing chambers in the stargate provide a light frequency that helps to accelerate and purify you. The healing chambers will also be able to raise your energy. Your coming into the stargate will involve entering a series of light chambers that will assist you in removing the densities and structural forms that would be considered burdensome.

Ideas and densities from previous incarnations are still in your auras, and they will need to be removed. You will need to be cleansed of negative energy patterns. Removal is not as simple as cutting something off. It is true that you can cut the cords of attachment to the Earth plane. However, you still have lingering scars in your energy fields that need to be purified. It is one thing to have the cords of attachment cut. It is another to be in a totally healing vibration that will allow you to enter into the fifth-dimensional realm, the realm of the Arcturian stargate.

We will also assist you through the stargate in another way. In the Arcturian system, our children are educated and trained in a manner that coincides with their own highest good and their individual mission. In the stargate, we can also provide this process for you. We can learn much about you, and assist you in your purification so that you can go to the proper area of the galaxy that is in alignment with your highest spiritual good.

ENTRY INTO THE STARGATE

The Arcturian stargate is now available to you through thought projection. You cannot go through the stargate until you complete this incarnation, but you may go to the stargate by means of thought projection, and view a multitude of choices. These choices are based on your frequency and your vibration. You can only enter certain gateways if you have achieved the vibratory frequency that comes with the lessons learned, that comes with your maturing and your integration of energy on the third dimension. Your frequency automatically determines which gateways you can enter.

It is known in the galaxy that one cannot even approach this stargate without the proper frequency. It takes a certain energy acceleration to approach the stargate. It requires a high level of spiritual energy. Still unknown to most human beings, spiritual energy is one of the most powerful and creative forces in the universe.

Your entry into the stargate will be the culmination of your ascension work. The ascension can be viewed as an acceleration and also as a skipping of several processes, a leaping ahead. You can consider this similarly to skipping grades in school. You may be in the eighth grade and then suddenly you will go to the tenth grade. There might have been experiences in the ninth grade from which you could have benefited, but the overall goal of graduating as soon as possible takes precedence over being in school any longer. When you come into the stargate, you are going to be in a process of acceleration. You may be skipping a lifetime or two. You are in a situation where you will need to advance quickly.

You have been waiting for many lifetimes to come to a position like this where you can go into a stargate and consciously direct your progression. As we have said before, access to the stargate is limited to those who have achieved a particular level of attainment. However, because of the acceleration and access to the ascension energies, your opportunity to go into the stargate will arrive at a much earlier time. You may think that you have many more lifetimes to go through, or many more lessons to learn. Fortunately, however, you are about to take a quantum leap.

Everything that is happening, everything that is moving toward this amazing phase of your planet can be viewed as an evolutionary leap. The evolutionary leap in consciousness is going to move you closer to that point where you can literally jump into the stargate. The ascension can be viewed as something in which you can move forward perhaps ten or fifteen lifetimes of work in a very short time by doing such intense work. By doing intense work, you are going to gain entry to the stargate.

Many channels throughout the country and the world are talking about "stargates." We are in the process of connecting many powerful grid points on the planet, especially in Mexico and South America, to the Arcturian stargate. Our vocabulary is somewhat different, because we do not refer to an opening, or vortex, as a stargate, but rather as a corridor. You can connect a corridor to a fifth-dimensional portal that will bring you constant energy from the stargate. The Arcturian stargate is only stargate in this section of the galaxy toward which we are all evolving.

People have asked if there is one particular place on the planet that provides a much better access to the stargate. Crestone, Colorado is now one of the most open areas in the world that connects to the Arcturian stargate. A very powerful corridor in the Crestone area will allow many people access to the stargate. We will work with you to enhance and amplify your access to the stargate.

Choosing Your Next Existence

The stargate is a gateway in the truest sense of the word: a gateway to the stars. This is, however, a simplistic explanation. It is a gateway to many different dimensions in the star systems. You can go through the stargate and use its energy to propel yourself into the next dimensional realm, the next planet, the next area in the galaxy in which you wish to go.

This stargate processing point can facilitate sending you to different planets, such as planets in the Antares system, or planets in the Pleiades, or even planets in another galaxy. You cannot go directly from one planet to another unless you pass through this stargate. You are beginning to see the importance of the stargate. If you wish to return to your home planet in the Pleiades, for example, and you are about to experience your ascension or even physical death, then you can project yourself through the stargate and into the Pleiades by direct link.

There are gateways that lead into other gateways. For example, one fifth-dimensional world gateway may take you to gateways in other realms in the fifth dimension. Other gateways could return you to some third-dimensional realms, such as Earth or other planets, only at a much higher vibrational level. You may even view another gateway that would offer you a choice of different galaxies, from the fifth dimension or third dimension. Your choices become arithmetically progressive.

We have many abilities on the stargate. With the permission we have been granted by Sananda and the High Counsel, we can even explore another Earth incarnation for you. If you have some unfinished work on Earth, we can direct you to the portal for you to actually observe that lifetime if you were to go back. By looking at that potential lifetime from the stargate portal, you could assimilate the lessons that were there without going into the incarnation. That is, Earth friends, high technology in the galaxy! We can do this because you are sincere in your desire to come to Arcturus and the stargate. There will be limited and difficult times ahead for the Earth, and returning for another third-dimensional lifetime would not be a very pleasant incarnation.

One of your choices is to come back to the Earth through the stargate. One of the portals does return to the Earth. If you choose to return to the Earth, this time, however, you will return as a fifth-dimensional being. A creative construction is currently underway for the Earth's fifth dimension. Rest assured that special places are being developed for you.

If one has graduated to the fifth dimension, and decides to return to the third dimension, then one must come back as an ascended master. None of you who are starseeds have previously resided in the fifth dimension totally. By that, we mean that none of the starseeds who are now on Earth have concluded their incarnation cycles, which would allow them to remain totally in the fifth-dimensional realm. As a starseed, you have only been exposed to fifth-dimensional energy in previous, non-Earthly incarnations.

The stargate is an important tool in bringing the Earth's fifth dimension into reality, because this requires an infusion of fifth-dimensional beings back into the Earth. Those of you who have been wondering whether or not you will be able to return to the Earth, you can first go to the new fifth-dimensional level of the Earth plane, and then you will be able to appear in the third dimension. This will make it more desirable for you to choose to return.

SOUL PROCESSING

Imagine that there is a processing place for your soul that puts you back into the incarnational process on Earth. You know that you have many different lifetimes in the Earth system. After each lifetime, you must meet your teachers, and process different aspects of your incarnation before you are directed to a new incarnation. The Arcturian stargate serves a similar function by processing you into different galactic planetary systems.

The Arcturian stargate is a sacred responsibility. Any work involving the soul, such as soul travel or soul processing, is recognized as sacred work. You may consider the stargate as a soul processing center. When you are working on this level, you realize the sanctity and holiness of this work. We want to make you aware of the holiness of the stargate. Many beings of the "Elohim" classification are there, among them being Archangel Metatron. Because we are dealing with

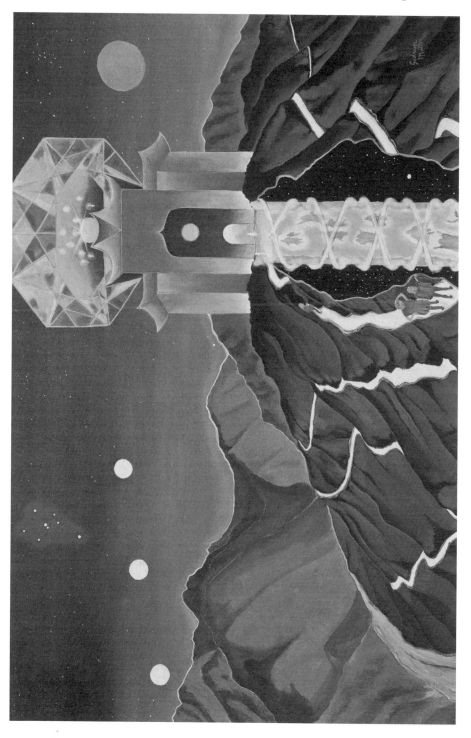

THE STARGATE

The Stargate was the first in the series of Arcturian images that came through for this book. It was the first painting I was asked to do by the Arcturians.

The Arcturians described the stargate temple as oriental in style, like a pagoda. It is on the blue-green planet of Arcturus with a yellow-green sun. A multidimensional corridor extends from Earth to the temple. Beings from Earth are moving up the corridor to ultimately transcend third-dimensional reality by moving through the stargate. There are three moons, and thus there is never total darkness. The Pleiades are visible in their sky. The Arcturians asked me to include all these details specifically, and expressed concern about my being able to get all these concepts onto one image. Included in the picture are Arcturians climbing the mountain path to the temple. Their planet is apparently very mountainous.

The stargate resembles a multifaceted jewel with gold overtones above the temple. After gathering information, guidance, and healing in the temple, beings move into the light as they pass through the stargate.

Gudrun Miller

decisions about soul travel and soul processing, many high beings are always present.

The Arcturian stargate has the function of being able to manifest heaven-like situations, such as meeting Metatron or other high angelic presences. The stargate will provide education, processing, and development for personal transformation, as well as the ability to proceed to the appropriate level and frequency for your next incarnation.

The tremendous amount of energy generated from the stargate is needed to process souls. Thousands, even millions of souls are always in process. We view this as one of the most important functions of our work. The stargate also has the function of introducing newly created souls into their first planetary systems. You can understand what a wonderful place this is, the center for processing incoming and outgoing souls for this sector of the galaxy.

Sananda is controlling or overseeing the group of human beings who will come from Earth through the stargate, or shall we say, who are approaching the stargate from Earth. Other beings, other Arcturians, other Pleiadians, others from different stars systems that you do not know the names of, are also assisting in introducing and directing those to the necessary corridors that lead to the higher realms. It is very important to understand the multitude of choices that you have before you come to the stargate. There is a major return chute to the Earth. Sananda is also overseeing that. Human beings will come up from the Earth, and return to the Earth as fifth-dimensional masters using this chute. Other ascended masters besides Sananda are working with us and assisting us as well.

This magnificent stargate is a huge operation, quite capable of simultaneously processing millions of souls. We have been working closely with Sananda in preparation for the huge influx of beings that will enter the Arcturian stargate during the ascension. We call on the energy of all of your teachers and guides to be with you and help you come into alignment with your higher purpose by focusing on your spiritual assignment and your evolution to the next level.

THE ARCTURIAN TEMPLE

The Arcturian temple is a preparation and purification area connected to the stargate. We must emphasize that you are currently bringing yourself to the point of being processed. In order to do this, you must essentially lose your ego. Your identity as an Earth being must be integrated because your higher self takes precedence. In the temple area, you can integrate your ego, lower self, and middle self with the higher self through a merging process. Therefore, you do not feel as though you are being shocked, and you do not sense a loss of consciousness. If you go through the stargate without processing, then you can lose consciousness. You must prepare for this higher transformation. It is especially beneficial for you to move through and work within the temple area.

Enter the corridor with us. Feel the pulsating energy as you move up the corridor to our ship, and enter into one of our healing chambers. We are now bringing a blue-white light to infuse in you a stepped-up energy. This light will bring you a new mental clarity. This mental clarity will give you a sparkling blueness about your aura that will help you to see what is occurring in your life with clarity. We seek to purify and cleanse your subconscious, and we seek to promote your conscious mental clarity.

We now bring to the center of the room a huge, beautiful blue and white crystal that has never been seen on your planet in physical form. We are allowing this crystal to descend in a chamber to the center of the room. You can participate by focusing your third eye as a beam of light into the crystal. Now you can interact with the crystal, and this crystal can bring you a special sense of peace and clarity.

The Arcturian mission is to assist you in the important aspects of your spiritual union with the stargate and your spiritual union with the Arcturian temple. This you can all do. No matter what density of problems you are experiencing, you can still come to us. Now we will ask you to merge your consciousness into this crystal.

Now see a magnificent temple on Arcturus before you, and then enter the beautiful Arcturian temple. It is a gigantic temple of blue light. You are here so that you may learn to be transformers for the ascension, and transformers of the Earth's energy fields. You are now receiving powerful light vibrations. We are working with your DNA energy, and we are working with your whole biological structure. You have an inner body and an outer body. Your outer body is what you see in physical presence on the Earth. We are working with you on your inner body. It is now going to be brought forth in light.

The Arcturian temple is a multidimensional structure. There are literally countless numbers of beings here. As you look around, you will be aware of others that are interacting, but not in exactly the same space. There are other people that are coming up here, other beings that are receiving this energy. Look up, and you see others actually going through the stargate, going to other star systems. You are not permitted to go through the stargate now, but look at the stargate from this position in the temple. You see that it is a beautiful, jeweled-like gate that is leading into many other realms throughout the galaxy. You can see through the gate, and can see others passing through the gate. As they go through, they are transforming, and they are leaving behind a sheath of their old body. They are dropping their old body with joy! It is a relief, a buoyancy, a new energy, a new light that is coming through.

Only those like yourselves who are becoming purified and of high etheric energy can even grasp the meaning of the stargate, and can begin to prepare themselves. We are going to activate your codes. We are working with you now so that you will be activated at the proper time. Now you are activated to come into an alignment with the energy of the stargate. That does not mean that you can go through it yet, but it does mean that you are receiving light and activation from the stargate. Receive this golden light from the stargate and the temple on Arcturus.

CHAPTER 12

THE CRYSTAL TEMPLE
OF TOMAR

This is Archangel Metatron. It is my purpose to guide you to your higher soul assignment in the realms that are awaiting you. Because time is not linear, you are already experiencing part of your awareness from this new assignment. You are multidimensional. You are simultaneously moving your consciousness in many different places. It is the wish of the Masters that you become aware of your multidimensional consciousness and multidimensional existence.

I will work with you to unlock your codes. Certain codes control your access to your past lives so that you are not flooded with memories that are too difficult, painful, or confusing. There are also codes that block your awareness to consciousness in other realms. These codes can be temporarily broken and lifted so that you can move your thoughts into the stargate.

I will go through several different incantations and then offer you tonal instructions. Finally, you will receive further instructions on how to enter these realms. We will begin first with *Kadosh, Kadosh, Kadosh, Adonai Tsevaot* (Hebrew for Holy, Holy, Holy is the Lord of Hosts). These words will unlock the first codes. Next we will go to the second level: *Eheyieh Asher Eheyieh* (Hebrew for I am that I am). May the codes that are locked be unlocked. May your consciousness be open to all soul assignments as you enter, in thought, the pre-chamber of the Arcturian stargate. This is Metatron.

THE CRYSTAL TEMPLE

We send you greetings from our Arcturian spiritual masters who are connecting with us, and who are wishing very much to send to you a powerful vision. It is a vision of spiritual beauty in a temple on Arcturus. This magnificent temple is built around and on top of a large lake. The outer temple structure is like a giant hexagon with a triangular point on the top. In the lake is a huge crystal that we are also connecting with. This crystal is a powerful doorway into galactic consciousness, higher dimensions, and past life memories.

This is Tomar, and I would like to take you to the Arcturian crystal temple. Come up in consciousness to one of our healing chambers on our ship. Now feel yourself spinning, and floating into a very beautiful, blue light. See a massive gateway before you. Countless numbers of souls like yourself are floating up to this beautiful gateway. Now we are going to spin again, and go up to the next level to the Arcturian crystal temple. We are in a huge, domed place on Arcturus used especially for healing. We also call this place the crystal healing chamber. As you are sitting on the edge of this wonderful place, you can see a huge crystal in the deep water. We manifested this crystal for special powers.

We still have maintained contact with your physical form. I want you to put both of your hands palm up, facing toward the center of the room. You are now in three places at the same time. You are in physical form on the Earth, you are in a healing chamber on our ship, and you are in the Arcturian crystal temple. We are very careful to integrate the healing work we are doing with you on all three of these levels.

We are inside the temple, sitting together, looking at the lake. We can see the beams and the power of the crystal that is in this lake. The lake is about a mile in diameter. The crystal is approximately a quarter of a mile in diameter, and is emitting a powerful light. Because it is so powerful, the water allows for a diminishing of the crystal energy so that people can assimilate it.

We cannot look at the crystal directly. We know that to look directly into the crystal without the water around it is to risk merging consciousness, and sending yourself immediately into another incarnation, which we do not wish for you to do at this time. We can, however, help you to safely look into this powerful crystal in the lake.

In this beautiful temple area, there is much chanting and singing. Several beings in white robes are with us, and other galactic beings are present that have come through this crystal energy. The crystal is an interdimensional aspect of the stargate that is located in the Arcturian Temple. This crystal is connected to the Arcturian stargate in a very interesting way. There are light beings from higher dimensions that frequently come through the crystal.

A powerful love energy is emanating from the crystal. It comes from a powerful, intergalactic force known as the Andromedan Council. The Andromedan Council is focusing a love energy for the emerging consciousness that we, the Arcturians, are working with. They are sending this love force to all who are meditating on this powerful crystal. They know it is the love that they send through this crystal that is the most healing for all on the Planet Earth. You are receivers of such a love force.

A STRAND OF LIGHT

This is Juliano. I would like to connect a mini-corridor, or a strand of light, from you to a fifth-dimensional opening in the crystal temple of Tomar. You will now have this connection with you twenty-four hours a day. That means that you will always have access to a fifth-dimensional perspective, and a fifth-dimensional connection in all of your activities. To possess this gift of light will enable you to be a much more powerful lightworker.

Now, specifically, how will this strand of light affect you in your daily life? When you have a fifth-dimensional perspective continually, you will have a new sense of detachment from third-dimensional activities, and you will be able to see them clearly from a fifth-dimensional perspective. You will also see how your third-dimensional activities can prosper, and benefit the movement of the whole Earth and the whole planetary consciousness to a brighter fifth-dimensional interaction. You will energize everything you do, everything you see, with this higher perspective.

Anything that you do—whether it be teaching, working as a sales person, counseling, physical labor, or just visiting your children—will be impacted by this new fifth-dimensional perspective. Every interaction will now carry this thread and allow you the opportunity to transmit that thread to other people. In all of your interactions, you will now be able to transmit a special frequency from the Arcturians in this fifth-dimensional strand. You will now become a powerful light, and people will be attracted to you wherever you go.

We will now transmit frequencies to you that will break the crystalline blocks around your aura so that you can receive more fifth-dimensional light. Now that you are more open, you can benefit more from our Arcturian light technology. This light technology will impact such areas as personal healing, unlocking your codes, transforming yourself into fifth-dimensional spaces, and your permanent ascension into the higher realms. This is our mission—to assist you in ascending to the fifth-dimensional realm. Our technology is very suited to this work.

Looking into the Crystal

This is Tomar, and you are my guests at the crystal temple. You have permission to participate in this marvelous crystalline energy. Gaze at the water with me now, and see the powerful ripples of energy coming from the crystal. Powerful energies are coming up from the crystal that are activating your telepathic powers, your third eye, and your crown chakra. They are also activating a huge energy infusion for you. Allow this energy to come toward you from this powerful crystal. Then, use the energy you have just received to look deeper into the water.

You may see a city on Arcturus called Arcturus One. As you are gazing into the crystal, you see people very joyfully in existence, in groups, having conversations, meditating, and joining in small family groups listening to others speak. Each Arcturian home has a powerful crystal for each member to use. This is our method of television. You are using your mass consciousness on your planet to engage in different visions through a television set that has limited value in terms of a spiritual enlightenment.

In Arcturus One, we have the ability to focus on special crystal structures. These are powerful crystals, but are not exactly like the crystal structures on your planet. We can gaze into consciousness, gaze into galactic energies. You are now able to do this, as you see many of the Arcturian families focus in this manner. Many are focusing on the Earth and are sending light and love to the Earth. Many are watching, and are very connected to the process. They are connecting as a group.

We look into the crystal and we see a great leader, a great spiritual presence, a high being in the galactic hierarchy that comes from the gardens of the Central Sun. We are receiving thoughts from this energy. You cannot interpret the thoughts at this point, but I am receiving thoughts as we are still in the temple with the beautiful lake and huge crystal.

I am receiving thoughts and information from the Central Sun energy. Go into that part of your brain that can infuse you with light. Some call this the pineal gland. Use that connection now to infuse light, to experience light. The pineal gland has an unbelievable ability to connect you to the light of the Central Sun. In the Arcturian brain, we have continual interactions with this area of our physical structure that is similar to your pineal gland. We use this almost as sustenance, as energy infusion. It is very difficult for us to imagine what it would be like not to have this connection. Indeed, we are sympathetic to your lack, at times, of being able to access this infusion of light that comes from within.

We continue to listen for other messages. Continue to work with the corridors, never underestimating their power. The corridors are perhaps the most advantageous ways for you to gain energy infusions from the Arcturians. Activate the corridors; meditate in the corridors.

It is important that each of you connect with your personal guardian, or counterpart, on Arcturus. You are ready in this learning situation and you will receive more personalized messages. We are very concerned that your evolutionary process on the Earth be as smooth as possible. We are infusing within you all with the light energy that I, Tomar, am receiving from the central crystal in the sacred temple on Arcturus.

Presently, there are many other wonderful beings in this beautiful temple. Hundreds of other beings are also here partaking of this energy and this powerful light. Many beings are absorbing this light into their third eye, using it for mental clarity. Because mental clarity is one of our highest goals and values, we are offering you guidance to activate your mental clarity. I bestow upon you an increased ray of violet and blue coming from our temple crystal to fill you with deeper mental clarity that will last for several weeks.

ENTERING INTO THE CRYSTAL

I would now like to help you enter deep inside the huge, underwater crystal. I will guide you into the crystal using thought projection. You will receive a very powerful jolt of energy that will accelerate your entire vibration. This will help you to feel transitory in the third dimension. We want you to understand that you really are transitory in the third dimension. It appears as if you are working in a dimension that is solid and permanent, but this is not the true reality of the third dimension. If you can attune to the frequency and the consciousness of the transitory nature of the third dimension, then you are going to accelerate much faster.

As we are sitting around the crystal, I want you to prepare your consciousness to go deep into this crystal with me. While I am floating above the crystal, I am going to take all of your hands. Do not try to understand this dimensionally, as it will not make sense. Each of you are holding my hand either on the left side or on the right side. Then we descend together into the crystal.

We are floating down deeper and deeper into the crystal. Now we are going to reach a point that may feel like half a mile down. We are deep into the crystal, and you continue holding my hand while we float here. We have arrived in a special fifth-dimensional palace that is in the center of the crystal. As we float here, we are going to absorb this very harmonious, etheric energy. I want you to plant your consciousness here in this golden palace of light deep inside the crystal. Another being is emerging to speak to you.

Greetings, I am T-Rahn. I am one of the spiritual masters of the Arcturian realm. I am blessing each of you, and I will personally connect your strand of light to this point in the palace inside the crystal. This is a golden palace filled with beautiful spiritual light and warmth, and everlasting etheric beauty and intensity. Please connect to this. We are so pleased that you are able to experience this depth of spiritual beauty from the Arcturians. We want more Earth beings to experience this Arcturian frequency. You are the forerunners in this grand experience.

The more that you can experience our Arcturian spiritual light, the more you will be able to spread this light when you return to Earth. This strand of light you carry will broadcast outwards when you go through your daily life. I go to each of you to assist your vibratory energy field as it is being accelerated so that you can continually have this frequency with you now, and as long as you need it. As Juliano and Tomar have said, there is every reason to celebrate now, for you will have this permanent strand with you. Because you have this connection, I am now sending a strong, blue tubular light into each of you. We are very pleased that you are able to receive this light.

Many great spiritual beings come here to gain energy before going out to other planetary systems. Sananda frequently comes here to be recharged. You are coming here for charging, as well. You will also return here to recharge, for you are becoming ascended masters. As ascended masters, you will be transmitting and delivering light throughout your daily interactions on Earth. This is T-Rahn.

This is Tomar. I will help you to return to the top of the crystal. Take a moment, and meditate with me now. As you are holding my hand, let us go back up to the top of the crystal. I will float back up and you will follow me. We go higher and higher, for it is a long way to the surface. Now we are at the top, floating above, and I send you back to a place around the crystal. You are now in a very good position to cement that strand of light so that it is permanently fixed from your Earth body to this place. Meditate on that strand, and connect it with your crown chakra.

EXPERIENCING YOUR LIGHTBODY

We use this crystal temple to help recover the total soul identification with the lightbody. There have been cases where people are not able to connect with their lightbody. They were not able to remember that their essence is the lightbody. Here, at the crystal temple, you may totally experience your lightbody.

I, Tomar, leader of the Arcturian spiritual community that is designed to work with Earth beings, call on the highest authority to bring your lightbody into the crystal temple. You will experience a light essence. Sense the power of the light energy coming from the crystal that is now in your proximity.

Your lightbody is neither male nor female; it is a soul essence. Begin to sense your lightbody being closer in proximity to the purified atmosphere forming the crystal chamber. Begin to feel your cellular structure becoming more open, and more excited. Here is the true opening that you have been wanting, the opening to your permanent essence, your spirit lightbody.

The spirit lightbody above you is connecting totally with the crystal in the water. I want you to look into the crystal with your third eye— not with your physical eyes, but with your third eye. As you look into the crystal, I want you to go deeply into it, not just on the surface of the crystal. You can go into a center point of the crystal considered to be as deep as one mile. Know that the deeper you go, the more you connect with this line of energy to your third eye and your lightbody.

Now, you have a triangle of energy that goes from your third eye deeply into the crystal and reflects back into the third eye of your lightbody. This is the beginning of the connection to your lightbody. Now we will work with your crown chakra. Connect a line from your crown chakra deeply into the crystal. That line will then resonate with the crown chakra on your lightbody. Do the same for your heart, solar plexus, sacral, and root chakras. Now you are connected with the next layers of chakras, and you are coming into alignment with your lightbody.

Some of the lightbody essence is slowly descending back into your physical body. Slowly absorb this vibrancy. Know that as this energy is coming into your physical body, you are becoming totally androgynous. Androgynous does not only imply male and female, but also refers to Earth consciousness and galactic consciousness. Your society is so focused on this distinction between the sexes, but know that you are also multidimensional, multi-identity beings—beings that have a dual identity, both as Earth beings and as space beings. This is a more comprehensive view of androgyny. As your lightbody descends into your physical body, you are becoming a galactic, androgynous being. This identity is being communicated down to your Earth body— the galactic, androgynous state of consciousness.

As you integrate your lightbody, you need to know that your lightbody is connected directly to the Creator source energy. From the crown chakra on your lightbody, you have a direct source of light from the Creator source and the Creator light. Each of us, including the Arcturians, has a specific energy connection to the Creator source that is unique. We learn from you as you learn from us.

The Creator light that you are experiencing is unique. This light holds a special message and a special frequency. Some of you will be able to translate that into a word, a tone, or verbal instructions. For example, some new messages could be: Light is Oneness; Light is Beauty; Arcturian Blue Light; Unifying Light; Being Light; Purifying with Light. Allow yourself to feel a message from the Creator source. Then, send this message and this experience down to your physical body on Earth.

Send the words or tones you have received to your physical body. On the third dimension, words and thoughts create. You can create a personal healing from this point by sending the proper words, tones, or symbols down to your physical self. This is the beauty that we have found in the third dimension: words can create. Send down words of love to yourself on the physical plane.

In your lightbody and in the crystal temple, you can travel to many different parts of the universe. You can travel to the Andromeda Council in our sister galaxy. The Andromeda Council is a group of light beings that has a close relationship with the White Brotherhood/ Sisterhood. In the Andromeda Council, there are powerful light beings, beings as powerful as Sananda-Jesus. The Council is very interested in your dimensional unification with your lightbody. From this place in the temple, I want you to think: "I am traveling to the Andromeda Council." I, Tomar, will be your escort as you travel to the Andromeda Council in our sister galaxy. One from the Andromeda Council now wishes to speak to you.

GURHAN OF THE ANDROMEDA COUNCIL

I am Gurhan from the Andromeda Council. We are specialists in light technology and lightbeings. Your coming to us with the assistance of Tomar is a true blessing for us all. You are bringing to us information and messages about your evolution from the Milky Way galaxy. We are a galactic council, which is set up to receive emissaries from your section of the Milky Way.

We communicate through light. We do not need to use words, but as we are working with you, we can facilitate your understanding through the use of words. Three beings on our council possess the spiritual quality and the power of Sananda. They are all related to the monadic energy of the One—perhaps what you might refer to as the Son of Man energy. There is a monadic force in our galaxy that is similar to the energy of Sananda.

We love your progress in evolution and transformation. My message to you is this: you are beginning to use your light technology, and you will grow in magnificent leaps and bounds. Light technology will not only help you to materialize and dematerialize, but will help you to thought project and heal your physical body. Eventually, you will move beyond physical existence. You will soon understand that physical existence is no longer necessary. It will be considered a burden, and you will leave that density behind.

We are excited to see that the Earth is preparing to receive her light essence, her lightbeing. When the Earth does this, she will then be in universal communication with all fifth-dimensional planets. On the fifth dimension, using the available light technology, you can instantly communicate with other planets without using cumbersome, third-dimensional technology such as radio waves.

There is no fear on the fifth dimension—none whatsoever. I, along with Tomar, will temporarily lift the fear from your cellular memory. Feel all fear temporarily removed from your cellular structure while you are in our light. Fear is third-dimensional. The memory of fear can now be temporarily erased while the love vibration is amplified. For every ounce of fear that left your body, let that place be filled with love.

We can appear as a flash of light in your dimension. There have been sightings of light from unknown sources reported by some of your workers. You cannot touch this light, capture it, or shoot it down. It is this light source that is creating the true crop circles. It is necessary to communicate to you in a nonverbal way which will bring you closer to light communication. On a higher level, it can be said that this is simply a light exchange. The crop circles contain codes within the imagery that will release fear from you in the third dimension.

I ask you to meditate on the crop circles. When you do so, think of the Andromeda council and our light technology. When you return to Earth, you too can use this special light technology. Visualize a star above your crown chakra that is radiating outward continually. Once you activate this star, you can connect with us, with the Arcturians, and with other light beings in the galaxy and beyond. Now I will return you to Tomar. This is Gurhan.

The Crystal Temple

The crystal temple lake is a mile in diameter with a huge crystal submerged in it. It is submerged in water in order to step down its power and protect those who come to the temple. The crystal radiates its own light, and illuminates all who come in contact with it. Beings from all over the galaxy and beyond gather on the shore for rejuvenation. Beings are able to go into the water and into the crystal with proper preparation and guidance. The temple walls are transparent, and there are many entrances. In the top of the dome is a three-sided pyramid.

Portraying the size of the crystal was a challenge for me. I found myself getting absorbed into the energy of the crystal, and easily could have let the crystal dominate the whole picture. The power of the crystal is so strong that I could see and feel its brilliance which is mostly in the form of light. The image I painted is truly a symbol to help others conceptualize the power and grandeur of the crystal.

Gudrun Miller

RETURNING TO THE EARTH

This is Tomar. We will now travel back to the Arcturian crystal temple. We will use this temple for a purification base. Look back into the crystal again and reactivate all your chakras. I remind you that it is important to have a Creator source affirmation to take with you from this work. Recharge that affirmation, and send it down to your third-dimensional body. The Creator source is always communicating. You must learn to receive and interpret this divine communication.

You can experience this integration from your lightbody in a deeper way. When your return to the Earth, there will be a shadow of your lightbody present. This is an indication that you have taken part of your lightbody down with you. The lightbody of your higher self is departing from your physical Earth presence, but it will have a shadow of itself around you. You can take this shadow with you for your third-dimensional presence.

We will now leave the crystal temple and return to the healing chamber on the Arcturian ship. The Arcturian spirituality is a very high form of light. By going into the crystal, you have experienced what is more of the permanent nature of your lightbody. When you look at your physical body on Earth, then you will know that it is more transitory. You will know that all of these things that you are doing, even the projects that you consider to be mundane, will present an opportunity to spread this fifth-dimensional light.

Take your consciousness back to your third-dimensional body now, and broadcast the fifth-dimensional light throughout all aspects of your life. We are assisting you in bringing this light into the third dimension. When you walk on the Earth with this light around you, you will be more sacred. Know that we, the Arcturians, always carry the sign and the shadow of our lightbodies. This is why we look so light and etheric to you.

Your next thirty days will be powerfully attuned to fifth-dimensional activity and fifth-dimensional immersion. This means that problems and blocks are now going to flow away for you. When you have the fifth-dimensional perspective, you must spread this light and use it to heal others. Each of you will now have a special healing ability. You might not think of yourself as a healer, but you will begin to have a healing affect on people. Healing is the true measure of fifth-dimensional light. This is Tomar.

A MESSAGE FROM KUTHUMI

Greetings, this is Kuthumi. I commend you on having successfully visited the Arcturian crystal temple in your consciousness, for you, my friends, are being trained to spread the frequency to others. First, you must feel it, you must experience it. This is what the service is about, the spreading of this frequency. You have a permanent connection, and the violet flame is deep within each of you now, burning and transmuting. I frequently come to the crystal temple myself. It is wondrous and delightful.

I am pleased that you have found avenues for your service in this mission. There is such a need to continually spread fifth-dimensional light. You may sense that others around you are blocked and have no hope. The fact that you carry the fifth-dimensional light will enter their aura. That is powerful in itself! If Sananda walked into this room, imagine his affect on you. He would have to say nothing; yet, you would be immediately transformed. That is all it takes—for Sananda to appear, and you will go to higher places. If you have a strand of fifth-dimensional light, then you will also affect others. Get ready for some wonderful interactions!

CHAPTER 13

PLANETARY ASCENSION

The ascension is a coordinated process that is occurring with assistance throughout the galaxy. The galaxy is multidimensional, and dimensional alignments must occur to coordinate the ascension. It is like your scientists have explained: this is an expanding universe. Everyone is in a hierarchical arrangement, and we are expanding and moving in that hierarchy. We have attained a special role in the expansion to assist you on the Earth plane. We know of the powerful interests and of the deep commitment that has been placed in the Earth ascension. We realize how many special beings and how many special interest groups are committed to the Earth. We know how many wonderful souls are here.

The more you expand in your spiritual wisdom, the more you are able to work in the higher dimensions. To work interdimensionally requires a spiritual growth and a spiritual graduation. We want you to understand that we are seekers of the highest spiritual light. Understand that everything is expanding, and we are expanding as well. We are moving to a higher realm and a newer light just as you are. This is a time of galactic transformation

Groups of very powerful beings are overlooking the evolutionary development of planet Earth. Clearly, huge numbers on the Earth are ready to move into a higher consciousness, ready to move up as a group. Some have referred to this as the number 144,000. This number was the number given at a certain point in history based on projections of how many people would be ready to move. Fortunately, that number is no longer correct. Many millions more are ready to move up as a group.

You are going to be part of a huge movement of energy that is coming. The galactic center is sending focal beings into the planet to provide more openings and more corridors for Earth. They will provide as many corridors as necessary, so that all who are ready can connect with the higher-dimensional realms. You have heard of the 26,000 year cycle of your solar system, and that you are reaching the 13,000 year mark. This creates a tremendous opening energetically.

The first ascension wave will be an opportunity for the planet to begin its own ascension process. This will be a beautiful experience. The planet is evolving as you are, namely, as a being that exists in different dimensions. The energy alignments that are occurring are just as important to the Earth as they are to you, for such energy can be very healing.

STABILIZING THE EARTH

Your planet can tolerate only so much, and then it will begin to spin out of alignment and seek a new balance. This is one of the reasons why so many from the extraterrestrial realm are coming to your planet—to send stabilizing energy to the Earth. Many of us are working with your planet to help it remain in balance longer so that you may continue your work.

We have experienced and witnessed planetary explosions, stellar explosions, collisions, and planetary shifts into other dimensions. There have been cases in our sector of the galaxy in which a band of lightworkers such as is now being developed on your planet, through a concentrated effort, brought a planet into another dimension so it could escape destruction. For that to occur, a critical mass of lightworkers had to exist. Your goal is not only to work toward your own ascension, but also to unite as lightworkers to bring about a planetary transformation. There is a need for lightworkers throughout the planet, not only in terms of numbers, but also in terms of their doing work in various locations. Certain parts of the planet need to be stabilized by interconnecting the grid areas.

On your planet, many have begun this process of linking the Earth to her interdimensional phase of transformation. This needs to be coordinated. At all times, people should connect the Earth to her new dimensional space. The concept of the connecting link is very important. We must work together with as many people as possible now to bring all lightworkers to a similar wavelength. You can focus and assist in the shift. Your chosen purpose as lightworkers is also to assist in the planetary transformation.

Preparing for the Ascension

You must actually prepare yourselves for the ascension. We will not give you weapons, nor will we beam you up at this point. You have no reason, however, to fear for food or safety. There is no need to be frightened or to arm yourselves. If any rescue needs to be accomplished, we will be able to assist you without the use of arms.

It is not a matter of whether you are totally prepared. What does count is that you are beginning to prepare. All who are working toward the ascension can be protected from catastrophes in a very special way. This protection comes from preparing yourself by raising your vibrations from the third dimension to the fifth dimension. You can do this by projecting your energy into a corridor. The corridors are interdimensional spaces. Did you know that when you are in a corridor, any third-dimensional weapons or third-dimensional catastrophes cannot harm you? You will always be protected. If, for some reason, you were not able to return to the corridor, then you could be taken to the fifth dimension.

Those of you who have been hearing tones and sounds are already picking up the telepathic communication that we have provided. The tones are our first line of communication. It is a way of preparing yourselves to receive more intense and more exact telepathic communications from us. The tones are also preparing you to align yourself and to bring you into a state where you can be open to higher dimensional energy.

You must cleanse, align, and release your third-dimensional self so that you can move into the fifth-dimensional realm and receive fifth-dimensional ideas, energy, and information. The tones help to block out third-dimensional densities so that you can move into this state. You can use the sound of the tones to bring you into a closer alignment. This also helps to block out all unnecessary information.

With the tones, you are now prepared to receive the frequency of the fifth-dimensional realm.

The energies of those in the higher dimensions are helping to create the atmosphere and vibratory fields to change your awareness. It is important not only that you elevate your vibrations, but also that you place yourselves in surroundings that encourage you to do so. When the environment is conducive to your own betterment, then it is easier for you to shift your consciousness. This alone tells you how important it is to choose an environment that enhances your vibration.

You have all been on this planet before in previous lifetimes. You may encounter different areas of power spots and corridors to which you made a strong connection in another lifetime. In previous lifetimes, you have been able to form a connection to a previous place that will activate your consciousness. It is only natural that when you return in another incarnation, you will want to find that same place again. You yearn to discover this familiar place again because you left an energy code or an energy signature there.

FIRST THE FOURTH, THEN THE FIFTH

It is true that the Earth is going to move into the fourth dimension over the next few decades, and it is true that most people will move into the fourth dimension as well. The Earth and its inhabitants are already in the process of transmuting into the fourth dimension. Many people will remain in the fourth dimension because they will not have the required spiritual energy necessary to ascend to the fifth dimension.

Starseeds, however, and those who can be activated toward this understanding, may skip the fourth and ascend directly to the fifth dimension. We want to emphasize that those who are not starseeds, those who are still rooted in the Earth's incarnational cycle, can still become starseeds in consciousness and ascend to the fifth dimension as well. The fourth dimension will still keep you in a realm where you are involved with Earth incarnations, and you will necessarily have to return to Earth. When you ascend to the fifth dimension, you will be free of the incarnational cycle, and you will only come back to Earth if you choose to do so.

The Earth will also go into the fifth dimension, but at a different time. The Earth may not go into fifth dimension, for example, until the year 2050. It may not be until a later point. Many different factors must occur for the Earth to totally transform. Much is going to happen before then, and the starseeds are all going to be physically long gone from the Earth plane.

Those of you who are starseeds and return to the Earth as ascended masters will be participating in the Earth's transformation into the fifth dimension. This transformation into the fifth cannot occur without the assistance of—and you will be astounded at this number—144,000 ascended masters who will be needed on this planet to move the Earth to the fifth dimension. It is an overwhelming task.

You can now understand the importance of the assistance of the starseeds, the importance of many of them having to return, and the importance of a core group to participate as ascended masters. This is where the importance of 144,000 comes in. Not that only 144,000 are going to ascend, that number is much too small. There are already almost three million people who are prospective "ascenders" into the fifth dimension.

MISSION OF THE LIGHTWORKERS

There will never be a majority of lightworkers on the planet in relationship to the population. We say that in relation to this current time period. Currently, the Earth has over six billion people. There will never be over three billion lightworkers. Can you imagine how fantastic it would be if there were that many lightworkers? How easy it would be to transform the Earth!

Presently, the number of lightworkers is probably closer to four million worldwide. The number of lightworkers that will actually leave the planet on the first ascension will be much smaller. We are estimating a number of about 250,000 to 300,000. You can see that this is not even 10 percent of the total lightworkers, and certainly a very small number when compared to the total population of the planet.

Those in control of the planetary resources and the military are very capable of exerting physical domination over the masses. How can the lightworkers have any lasting effect on this situation? What is your real role as a lightworker? We are here to remind you of your number-one job: to assist in preparing the Earth to be born into the fifth dimension. You are also here to awaken and activate others.

The energy exchange of moving from the third to the fifth dimension requires an overwhelming burst of energy. The interaction of the lightworkers with the Earth can be compared to a burst of energy from an atomic reaction. You can indeed be a channel for huge bursts of energy into the planet. However, in order to be a channel for this type of energy, you must be totally pure and totally in alignment. Were you to be out of alignment and then try to transfer that type of energy into the planet, the results would be very uncomfortable for you. We encourage you to work on clearing your personal problems so that you may become a channel for bringing this fifth-dimensional energy into the Earth. We know that you are still experiencing clearing, but you are at a point where you are going to be able to bring in more energy.

The energy that comes into you can be emitted through you. Receive the energy through your crown chakra and send it out in a burst, or stream, from your heart chakra to the Earth. This very powerful exercise will bring you into a new alignment and to your true path and your true mission. Many of you have questioned for months: "What am I supposed to do?" We will tell you, it is a combination of your personal purification, and the transmitting and emitting of this energy. We are above you in a special vessel that is receiving powerful energy from our mother ship. On this mother ship are ten Arcturian spiritual workers who are directing energy to us while we are directing it to you. This light energy we are sending is blue and silver. Because it is a high-speed energy, you cannot hold it for a long period of time. You are being trained to carry this energy and hold it, perhaps for as long as five to ten seconds. Then it will dissipate. That's why it is important that you redirect it to the Earth as soon as you can.

BUILDING A BRIDGE TO THE FIFTH DIMENSION

Our actual planetary mission is to assist in the stabilization and transformation of the Earth into the next level. Your mission is to fulfill your role as a star being on the planet. Some of you acknowledge that you have within you the consciousness of having previously been a star being. We are depending on you to help build the bridge to the fifth dimension.

The connection to the fifth dimension that the Earth has now is so powerful that beings who are on other planets are now attracted to the

Earth. This means that other planets exist in the third dimension that are solely devoted to spiritual growth, but the souls there still need the dimensional experience on Earth to complete their tasks. Many need to provide a service through the Earth experience that will help them to generate the necessary spiritual energy for ascension. This is what each of you are trying to do now. You are seeking to raise your spiritual energy so that you can ascend into the next realm.

How are you going to build and stabilize this bridge to the fifth dimension? The first answer is that you need to build a bridge for yourself. We are offering you a personal bridge to our consciousness through our work with you and through our corridors. As you cross over this bridge, you must ask yourself: How am I going to provide a bridge for others? How am I going to provide the bridge for my daughter, my son, my husband, or my friend? They may not be open to this bridge. You must learn to provide information and ways to this bridge in a manner that they can comprehend.

We have toned down, or stepped down, our explanations to you about the Arcturian work so that you can more easily understand and accept these concepts. Now, you must step down the information to others so that they can understand it. We are not talking about going out on the streets and trying to convert people. Connecting with others in a group provides a powerful access to this bridge. Certainly you need reminders that the fifth-dimensional energy is slowly beginning to seep into your lives. It is wonderful to see this occur now. Be aware that this fifth-dimensional light is coming down to you and can be received through your crown chakra.

DISCHARGES THROUGH THE CORRIDORS

Many of you will be contributing to the discharge of negative energy. This is very important. Because you are capable of activating different places, you also have the opportunity to discharge powerful energies. Understand that when you work with this energy, it is an opportunity to provide a healing for your planet. We can handle the negative forces on the Earth, and we continuously assist in the dissipating of negative energy. The more corridors we have open, the more connections we have with the Earth, and the more we can allow for discharges of negative energy. When this energy is discharged, the likelihood of catastrophic Earth changes lessens. This is what lightworkers are about, not only to provide models, but also to provide assistance in the planetary transformation. This can be seen in the work of Dr. Norma Milanovich, (author of *We, the Arcturians*), who has traveled to different countries all over the world to activate corridors. Once these corridors are activated, there can be continuous discharges of negative energy.

If the energies of the Earth come more into a balance, then the Earth can hold and absorb more energy so that violent reactions do not occur. The energy releases, however, can be established only in areas where there has been a receiving of higher energy. You must have a vortex and an activation first, and then the discharge will follow. Other energies in the Earth along the electromagnetic grid lines can also be brought to this place of discharge and released.

Remember that the Earth is receiving higher light and energy from your work. The more corridors that exist along the grid lines, the more opportunities there are for releases. To activate the planetary grid lines so that the galactic energy can come through is very powerful and very healing for the Earth, and for you. You can do this!

GALACTIC AND GAIA SPIRITUAL ENERGY

This is Tomar. A special temple is being prepared for you on our ship. We are bringing you to a temple in one of our larger, more powerful mother ships. We are all sitting together in this beautiful temple on our mother ship located in the dimensional corridor between Jupiter and the other outer planets. Look around, and see the Earth from the perspective of Jupiter. It looks like a star—a bluish star planet. Come into our temple.

We have prepared a golden garden for you. One of our special crystals is in this garden. It is a bluish-green crystal that mimics the power and the energy of the Earth. It has the bluish glow of the Earth. As you see the Earth from outer space, you see her blueness. This crystal is emitting this blue light from replicating the pure energy of the Earth spirit. As we are sitting in the circle, place your hands over this crystal and absorb the perfect blue light energy from this crystal. Because this is the pure light of the Earth, you will be returning with this pure light within your body, and you will implant this light back into the Earth. This is what you love, and why you chose to come to the Earth. This energy is of your highest nature. We are helping to stabilize this pure light from the Earth.

Come to another part of the temple, and we will sit in a circle. There is another beautiful crystal inside the center of the circle that represents the spirit of the Galaxy. This crystal has never been shown before to Earth beings like yourself. Put your hands over the crystal. This crystal can only be described as a powerful shade of white that has never been seen by humans. It is not the pure white that you are used to seeing. This is a special galactic white. This crystal represents the heart and spirit of the galaxy.

My dear Earth friends, I am very pleased that you come to connect with the spirit of the galaxy. She is our mother. Just like the Native Americans view Earth as their mother, you will learn that it is the galaxy that is the great mother of us all. Your souls were born in this galactic structure called the Milky Way. Perceiving the Milky Way as your mother enables you to connect to the light of the galactic Central Sun. You can immediately be in contact with many higher beings in this galaxy.

As you held your hands over the crystals in the temple, you were receiving the coded vibrations to carry back to the Earth. I ask you again—hold your hands over the crystal of the galactic spirit, and draw the energy in. I am going to switch you now to the crystal of the Earth. Take that vibration in. You have the pure energy of the Gaia spirit coming into you. You will carry this frequency back with you to Earth.

Once again, lightworkers, you are serving a powerful service, a powerful mission. The corridors are very important in all aspects, for the corridors that we are working with now, the Arcturian corridors, are serving several functions. First, you can come into the corridors; you can be pure in thought, and fifth-dimensional in experience. Second, we can send down special energy that will help to stabilize the third dimension.

We love your third dimension. It is a wonderful teaching facility. Please spread this message, how wonderful is the school of the third dimension. We now return to the Earth, and we remain overhead.

CREATOR ENERGY AND THE PLANETARY SHIFT

Questions have risen concerning our role in working with the Ascended Masters. We are part of a special galactic ambassadorship that is focusing on helping others, like yourselves, come into an alignment with the higher dimensional energy corridors that exist not only on your planet, but also throughout the solar system. Our local galactic sector is a highly charged area containing many different planetary civilizations. The entire focus of our galactic sector is on the Earth at this time. This is why so many entities and beings are coming here. Your galactic sector is the "place to be," because when such a shift occurs, there is an opening in the Creator that allows others to experience the Creator energy in a new and divine way.

We all come here in service, but we are also coming to learn. We are here to experience the new opening that will come to the planet Earth. It is difficult for you to understand, for you will think that there will be a denser closing, or collapsing, of energy due to the changes, the potential devastation, the upheavals that are going to occur. Despite the truth of that description, we know from previous observations that this open ing to the Creator is available because of the phenomenal amount of energy that is being discharged from your planet due to the planetary dimensional shift.

You will all be very aware that you will be able to experience the Creator Energy in a new way, a way that will be desired by other beings. This is why many have come into incarnation now, to experience this opening. I must emphasize that this is an exciting and new experience for all of us, not just for you on the Earth. We know that there will be a moment of extreme challenge and extreme light where a new facet of the Creator spirit will manifest. We from Arcturus would travel anywhere in the universe to be here with that kind of energy. We are spiritual beings like yourselves, and we are in pursuit of higher knowledge of universal love and universal energy. We wish to be close to the Creator, we wish to be of service, and we seek the new openings that are now available here. You may call it a crack in the dimensional framework.

Many of you are working very hard to complete much karma and service. What you are doing is very important and very needed. Those who are being healers to others, you are on a deep mission of service, and this mission is a wonderful opportunity to also be closer to the Creator opening that is about to occur. So those of deep service are, in a sense, experiencing a special opportunity to be close to the wonderful Creator opening that is coming. We are all very excited to be a part of this opening. All the Groups of Forty will be aware on a deeper level of this special opening, and you are all going to be very powerfully involved. We are preparing you through our vibrational work to raise your energy so that you can consciously experience the wonder and the joy of the interdimensional transformation.

The new Creator opening has not been described nor seen by anyone. Not even the ascended masters know the exact tone, frequency, and color of the opening. So you see, it is exciting for us as well. We only know that a special and unique vibration-color frequency is going to be descending on the Earth. We of other dimensions have all been on planets that have experienced a Creator opening, and we know how revitalizing, exciting, and wonderful it is when such an opening occurs. The Earth is very close to this time, very close to experiencing this energy. Some have asked if this will be associated with the ascension. We can only say that this is a matter that will only be revealed in the final moments of the opening. Many other planets in this sector of the Milky Way galaxy have gone through this experience. Each is unique, and each is very informative of the Universal Creator Energy Field Mind.

ONENESS WITH THE CREATOR ENERGY

Have the thought of oneness as you listen to our words and our tones. Send out your energy; send out your light to all people. Connect even higher, so all are moving to the connections with the Arcturians and with our ship. We are sending out a beam of light to be an attractor of energy. You can picture beams of light coming out from the ship we are in, creating a huge circle that is unifying all of your energy. Underneath that circle, there are further individual light beams going out. Hold that connection. You are going to experience thoughts as if they were part of you, although these thoughts are coming from the Arcturians.

Listen to our thoughts now. Focus on the connection your higher self has with the Creator energy. The highest striving in the universe is to be able to comprehend and experience the light of the Creator. We are one with you. Feel our energy. Feel the love that we have for all of you. Feel oneness with the galactic presence. Understand that just as there is a spirit presence of the Earth that you call Gaia, there is also a spirit presence of our galaxy that you know as the Milky Way galaxy.

We connect to the spiritual light of our galaxy. The Arcturian stargate is connected to the galactic consciousness.

CHAPTER 14

HUMAN ASCENSION

It is important for you to mentally understand what is going to happen in the ascension process, and what is happening now. You will find that we are very excellent resources for you. We can provide mental clarity on many of these issues. We have worked with you to assist you in gaining mental clarity. We will continue to work with all who read this information to improve their mental clarity, for it is only with total awareness and total mental clarity that you can pass through the stargate. This is not something where you are going to totally lose consciousness. You are going to experience a total understanding of many things.

There is a yearning throughout the world and throughout the country for the extraterrestrial, higher-dimensional energy. You know that you need this, just like you need food and water. You need the stimulation from us, or from other higher beings to generate your spirituality, to accelerate your electromagnetic fields. These contacts are deepening your awareness of the forces that are coming to you on planet Earth and the forces that are already on the planet.

The time will come when it will be necessary for you to look for us in the skies. You must deepen your concentration when you look toward the sky. You will begin to see streams of light coming from a certain sector of the sky. The contact with us will be important to you. It will be a necessity for your development. You will need the light and the contact to continue to successfully maintain yourselves on the planet Earth.

Quite frankly, the planet is in an overwhelming state of chaotic forces that are crisscrossing the meridians on the planet. The struggle to keep an ongoing sense of order is becoming more and more difficult. This sense of order that you know as your day-to-day existence is very fragile, more fragile than you are aware of. Perhaps you have become aware of its frailty when you see some of the chaos being manifested in catastrophes. You may ask yourself: How do I prepare? How do I bring myself into alignment?

You must put your priorities into correct order. It is this spirituality, this spiritual light work that is before you that must have the highest priority. That is your intention, that is your goal, to deepen your spirituality, to heighten your energy fields, your receptors, your intentions, your concentration toward the goal of a spiritual, dimensional shift. You are going to move into the fifth dimension. There is no doubt about this, and it is no small matter.

If you are depressed, you have a low energy field. Being around someone who is depressed can slow you down. In a normal mood, your energy is vibrating quickly, but in an accelerated energy, you must be even faster. It is not that your mind is going to process faster, we do not want you to be confused about this. The frequency is higher, but the thoughts are not necessarily faster. In fact, in many instances, the thoughts actually slow down or stop. We call this wave technology, or thought technology. We wish to teach you more about using this technology to accelerate yourselves. The focus of a spiritual group is a wonderful way to increase your individual frequency.

TRANSITION TO THE FIFTH DIMENSION

Many starseeds will go to the fifth dimension. One assumes, though, that some will not be able to make it to the fifth dimension, and may only be able to go into the fourth dimension. As ascended masters who make it to the fifth dimension, you can return to the Earth and assist her in her transformation. It will be your free will to do so, whether you choose to do it when the Earth is in the third dimension or when she is in the fourth dimension. Surprisingly, your assistance will not be as needed when the Earth is on the fourth dimension. We predict that many of you will only be interested in assisting the Earth when she is in the third dimension.

Many of you will not be as attracted to the Earth when she goes to the fourth dimension. There will be another energy magnification on the Earth, and you will not be as needed as you are now. You are primarily assisting the Earth in helping her go from the third to the fifth. If and when the Earth goes into the fourth, you will not have the same powerful role in the Earth transformation from the fourth dimension into the fifth.

Hope still remains that the Earth can go from the third dimension directly into the fifth. It was hoped that the Earth could make the leap. Frankly, it is all that can be done now to hold the Earth together in the third with the tremendous destructive energies that have been unleashed on your planet. There has not been a lot of discussion about the fourth dimension simply because most of you want to be free of all Earth incarnations and entanglements. In the fourth dimension, you are not totally free of those entanglements.

You should only have one goal: the total transformation of your physical existence to the fifth dimension, to the stargate, where you will be able to move through portals that will direct you to the appropriate planetary experience. Bring your consciousness to a higher place now—to a place where you can be above the Earth in consciousness and be in a wave of energy. You are waves of energy just as we are. You are magnificent in your full embodiment. Your full embodiment extends at least twenty feet around you. It is time to expand your awareness. Go in your thoughts and move to a point of consciousness that includes a twenty-foot perimeter around you.

You are coming to a point in your consciousness where you are going to begin to see into the fifth dimension. You are going to be able to experience new visual lights, new visual cues. With the chaos and the conflicting energies on the planet, lightworkers have a mission to bring order, meaningful actions and meaningful interpretations to what is occurring, and to devote your life to the transformation into higher consciousness. We recommend that it is time to drop many of the material endeavors that have no spiritual meaning to you, that have no real or lasting value.

Your thought processes include your ability to visualize and understand where you are going. You are doing very well with this. Many of you are correctly incorporating thoughts that have to do with the ascension and accessing the higher planes. Remember that who you are has to do with understanding yourself as a galactic person, and as an electromagnetic being of light. These are proper concepts. But there is one more concept we want you to understand: you are a being in the process of transition. This is an inherent part of your path. This can also be interpreted as: you are a being of expansion. Because you are beings of transition and expansion, you resemble the Creator energy, which is moving to expand through the inner work of those who are part of the family of the Creator. It is the law of the Creator to expand. Our expansion is following the command of the Creator energy.

Many of you wonder about where you are going to go when the ascension occurs. You wonder whether it will be Arcturus, or the Pleiades, or somewhere else. Please keep in mind that the stargate is the first goal. We would say for you to focus on going to the stargate. You will have all the time you need to integrate once you have reached the stargate. Not only do you need to integrate your Earth incarnations and all that has occurred on Earth, but you also need to integrate your incarnations from other planets. Part of the process is integrating the Earth incarnations, or the Earth energy, with the Arcturian energy. Since the Arcturian energy is a pure frequency, you will always be pro tected when using this frequency. There will be no intrusions, for example, from the Grays, negative Orions, or negative Sirians. You will experience no loss of control. Because we are pure spiritual beings, we have no desire, no interest to corrupt or control you. We are only interested in helping you develop a heightened frequency and a heightened state of love.

An Energy Boost Is Needed

As you move into fifth-dimensional energies, you will gain the ability to comprehend and to work with interdimensional and inter-universal energies. Between this current time period of 1997 and the approximate time period of 2020 to 2030, there will be available a special grace, a special compensation, and a special energy. A large boost of spiritual energy will be made available to you. This boost of energy is going to give you the vibration and the energy level to leap to the fifth. It is true, however, that if you have certain types of unresolved karma, you might not be able to jump to the fifth dimension. You cannot skip lessons.

How is it then that you will be able to skip dimensions and move from the third to the fifth dimension? How is it that you will be able to move out of your Earth incarnational cycle? The only way that you can do this is through a huge energy boost. Moving into higher levels requires energy. We are not referring to the traditional energy that you know on the third dimensions, such as nuclear energy, or energy that you use to propel your cars. We are now talking about spiritual energy. We are talking about the energy that has to do with the higher self.

A specific energy level emanates from each human being. When you first meet a person, you can easily take note of their energy level. Each person vibrates on his or her own energy level. We notice that sometimes you are depressed, which would be considered a slower energy. If you are excited, you seem to have a great deal of energy. At other times, you are spiritual and feel much lighter. When you are in the state of highest spiritual energy, you will feel extremely light and you will have the ability to move yourself into the next dimension.

You will be required to have a certain energy level to move to the fifth dimension. This energy boost is being made available to you through the grace of Sananda-Jesus. When the energy boost comes, you will be able to process and work through a great deal of your karma and personal issues. Some may have personal issues that would normally take three or four lifetimes to process. However, with the help of these energy boosts and divine grace, you will be able to work through your issues in a very short time. Such shortening of your karma, which results in intense personal issue work, can cause hardships and problems for you. Part of our mission is to assist you in working with these energy boosts.

Your heart chakra is beginning to open, and this will be the key to your transformation. Do not focus so much on trying to mentally understand this aspect or that aspect. But understand that your heart is the key for your total transformation. Your heart is very comfortable with this. Your heart is very knowledgeable, and knows exactly how to align for your ascension.

We want you to know that many guides, teachers and angels are present to help you. We work with Sananda, Mother Mary, Kuthumi, El Morya, Quan Yin, and many other ascended masters. Our Pleiadian friends and many other extraterrestrial brothers and sisters are gathering here to help create a profound energy. We are creating a marvelous portal opening to the higher realms. Come into that portal and expand your consciousness!

It is only natural to expand your consciousness. Consequently, we are saddened by the contractions that we see our star brothers and sisters experiencing on the Earth. We know the difficulties that you experience. The loss of contact with the star fleet and the loss of contact with universal consciousness has been very hard for you. We compare this situation to being without food and water. This is how seriously we would experience being cut off from this consciousness. You now have, however, a wonderful opening and opportunity to reconnect with this energy.

THE POWER OF GROUP SOUL ENERGY

Because we are more tied in with the group energy and the group soul energy, we are able to live longer. Even your species was able to live for hundreds of years as recorded in your Old Testament. Now it is unusual for someone to live beyond eighty-five years, even though you have the biological ability to live much longer. The reason is simply that you have not developed the technology of groupness and multidimensional awareness. In order to live for longer periods of time, you must have deeper connections with other dimensions.

You cannot maintain an existence for a long period of time without contacting the higher realms, for your bodies will wear out too quickly. The key to extending your lifetimes and good health is first to focus on higher-dimensional energies, and then to bring those energies down into your physical bodies. Without this ability, there is no way a being can live beyond the expected lifetime of eighty or ninety years. We are able to live as long as ten thousand years.

In your development, you are now working with the individual soul and the group soul. This is a very powerful point. You will understand, as we have, that in order to make the next evolutionary step, you must do it as a group. Based on our information about your ascension, this is very important. In fact, much of the success of the ascension will rely on group energy. You know that the guides and teachers have talked to you about waves. The waves will be groups, not primarily individuals. Although individual ascensions have occurred, ascension will generally be a group process. Those of you who are not as developed as some of the ascended masters would not be able to ascend were it not that you were participating in a group experience.

So we are very interested in the relationship between the individual soul and the group soul. This is one of the illusions of your existence in the third dimension—that is, your experience of being separated from your soul family and from your soul group. It is a great burden to feel separated, and many are overcome with anxiety. On the other hand, many have taken the other path, and have totally turned themselves over to the group. They have then lost their individuality and their free will. We are aware of these individual problems of will. We have also struggled with balancing issues of the will for a long time.

REACTIVATING YOUR GALACTIC CONSCIOUSNESS

It is true that there is much work for all to do in the times ahead. The work you are going to do will be lighter and easier because you are going to connect with your galactic consciousness. You left part of yourself behind when you incarnated on the Earth. You left behind that part of your self that relates to your sense of galactic consciousness. Each of you has a starseed element within you that is connected to the basic core of the galaxy. We Arcturians are living on that thread of consciousness continually. We resonate with the galactic core on a continual basis. It is an energy vibration that helps us to remain in the spiritual state that we so desire for you. You will connect with us more effectively and make better use of our contact by simply realizing your galactic heritage and reactivating your galactic consciousness.

One way to reactivate your galactic consciousness is to simply focus on the star Arcturus in your meditations. See the star in your consciousness as you stargaze, and then meditate on the star. Many of you will be able to send your energy and your thoughts to the star. Arcturus will bounce the energy back to you. Have you heard of a moon bounce? This is a technique that your radio technicians use when they send a signal to the moon, and it bounces back from a different angle. A radio signal can be sent from San Francisco to London by bouncing the signal off the moon. When you send your thoughts to the Arcturus system, they will come back to you with energy from us, and energy from some of our elders who have chosen to work with you now.

We have groups of elders that are now coming together in our temples. They are open to communicating with many of you now. They are open to receiving your thoughts and requests, and they are open to sending you information and energy from the Arcturus system. This is a different energy than the energy that you would receive from our space ships. The energy that is coming from Arcturus is of a special etheric rate and vibration.

It is extremely important for you to be in acceptance of your galactic heritage and your galactic consciousness. You must also realize that the personal problems you are engaged in can be facilitated through receiving this higher light from the Arcturian system. You will gain in spiritual wisdom, and you will be able to use that wisdom to resolve the particular problems that each of you have. You will then consider these problems, such as financial or relationship problems, to be minor compared to the overall goal of your soul development and the process of moving into this higher realm.

Your acceptance of your galactic and star heritage is essential to your ascension process. You must believe in something before it can become a reality. When you believe in your galactic heritage and your galactic consciousness, you will activate your starseed. This activation will allow you to remember, in a very positive way, your past-life connections as a star being. Once you have done this, you will begin to connect with others of like mind, and you will realize your importance in the events to come. Each of you now has a particular energy and a particular uniqueness and perspective that is needed.

On our world, many Arcturian groups are continuing to telepathically connect with human beings on the Earth. Groups on Arcturus meet regularly to send out messages to reawaken the lightworkers on Earth. All who are reading this, we send out a beam of light to all of your third eyes. Hear the sound of a hand clap, and receive the beam of light into your third eye. We are reaching a place where we will communicate with you not only by words, but also by light, energy, and tones. Absorb as much light as you can into your third eye. You need to ground this energy into the Earth as much as possible. You have been activated; your psychic powers and your psychic vision have been widened. Your frequency has been increased.

USING THE STARGATE ENERGY

This is Juliano, and we are the Arcturians. Our enthusiasm is very high in working with those who are so dedicated. It does not matter the level of spiritual development that you feel that you have attained. Some of you do not feel very spiritually evolved. Some of you feel that you are not good enough in your spiritual practices or your spiritual development. This is not a factor at all for us in working with you. We greet you because you are open, you desire to improve, and you want to bring your vibrations to a higher level that would enable your movement to the next dimensional realm. We are working with you so that you can enter the stargate.

You are moving to a place where you can become a being who can leap in consciousness. You will be able to leap over incarnations. In many cases, you will be able to leap over twenty to thirty Earth incarnations if you not only make this deep connection with us, but also open your consciousness to the stargate. Therefore, when you go through an ascension or any transition in consciousness, we want you to have the stargate in your mind as a place to reach.

We ask you to bring the stargate into your dreamtime. You will be amazed at how powerfully you can move in consciousness if you bring the image of the Arcturian stargate into your dreamtime. One of our main tasks is to introduce our existence into your consciousness on the planet and to introduce the stargate. The stargate is a powerful activator. It is a beautifully adjoining aspect of the main Arcturian temple on the planet, Arcturus. You can approach the stargate in your meditations, but you will only be able to go through the stargate when you are completing your Earth incarnations.

We will now bring down a powerful beam that fills the whole room with blue, gold, and white light. At the same time, we center the same beam on you. With the powers bestowed upon us under the authority of Sananda, we bring you up to our ship. With permission granted to us by our highest teachers, we can now allow you to come to the entranceway of the Arcturian stargate so that you may experience the power of the stargate.

See yourself before the Arcturian stargate in a beautiful garden. As you look over to the stargate, you see the powerful transformations of people entering the stargate from other parts of the galaxy. This stargate is not just for humans, or the Adamic race, but for others who are also reaching this point. Know that there are parallel developing planets that also have the Adamic codes, just as yourself. These beings are reaching a point of evolution so that they can process through the stargate as well.

You are under my special energy, my special protection. You are permitted to gaze at the light of the stargate. This is a special opportunity that you have. Only under the highest authority are you allowed to participate in the observation of this sacred place. Feast your eyes on the stargate. Observe the wonderful light and the power of this light in your aura. You can now bring this energy back down to the Earth.

You are so instrumental in introducing the energy of the stargate. All of you are in a position to leap in consciousness. I want to bring you into one of the temple rooms that is near the stargate. You may want to explore telepathic communications on a deeper level here. Some of you will receive colors before words. We send the color green to you now. We are now sitting in the temple room, and Tomar, a master from the Arcturian light chamber has emerged.

INCREASING YOUR LIGHT QUOTIENT

I am Tomar of the Arcturians. I greet you, and welcome you to the healing chamber in the Arcturian stargate temple complex. Your mission is to activate the energy of the Arcturians on the Earth and to use that activation to allow you to leap in consciousness to this point. Understand that you are being brought here to the temple, and that this is an assurance of your work as a starseed. Only as a starseed, and only because you have had such previous contacts, are you able to commit your light energy to this higher place. We continue to bathe and cleanse you with the healing light from this light chamber.

We now place a new energy octave in your aura. Assimilate this octave, for it is a higher octave of energy that will facilitate your leaping in consciousness. This is my message to you through Juliano. Understand this leaping ability that you have. The beauty of the Adamic race is that you are able to dramatically shift in consciousness. Now, what do you need to do back on Earth in order to leap?

Use the music of Mozart as we have instructed before. Mozart, an Arcturian starseed, received much of his musical inspiration from the temples here. Listen to this music as much as possible for one week. Open your hearts as wide as you can to all. Love and share with everyone. Call on me, Tomar, and I will be with you to help solidify this octave in your consciousness. Now I will bring you back into the garden and return you to Juliano.

Greetings, this is Juliano. We have more to say about the concept of a light quotient. Your light quotient, or light frequency, must be increased. You must ask to be given the ability to increase you light quotient on all levels. The key to ascension is in your light frequency. To increase the light frequency, you can ask for help from Sananda-Jesus, from the Arcturians, from Archangel Michael, Archangel Metatron, and from your personal guides. You can ask that your light energy quotient be increased in a way that you can presently assimilate.

Each of the masters and guides we just mentioned has a particular type of frequency that can be brought to you. The Arcturians can offer you a frequency that is truly different from that of Archangel Michael or others. You should request an increase in your light and vibration that will bring you to the next level that you need to be at. This could involve different levels and different bodies, such as the emotional body, physical body, or spiritual body. I do ask that when you wish to bring in a heart light energy, you go directly through the heart to Sananda-Jesus or to the Native American masters. The Native American masters have the permission, authority, and blessings of us all to work with the opening of your heart chakra.

CHAPTER 15

FORTY GROUPS OF FORTY

Not only can we view you and where you are going, we can also see your thoughts. It is very easy for us to see what is going to happen to you. We can see your whole life before you. We see how you are going to process everything, and we see so many of your connections. We also see you connecting to the fifth dimension. We see your higher processes, as well as your lower processes. We are able to follow and predict so much about you. We can see your very soul connections. We are delighted to see you, however, because you are very activated and very light. Those who do not have a connection to this light appear dark and contracted to us. When we see you and others like you, we see bright light and expansive energy.

You are drawn to us for many reasons. Some of you, as you already suspect, are Arcturian in your soul. You have been on Arcturus in previous lifetimes, and have agreed to come to Earth for your mission work, or starseed work. Just as some of you might go overseas to do a Peace Corps mission, starseeds from Arcturus have volunteered to come to the Earth plane on a mission. Now you are able to reawaken fully to your mission. Part of your mission involves aligning your frequencies to us. This enables a connection to be made that will help us to raise the overall vibration of your planet.

Some of you are not actually Arcturian starseeds, but you are evolving, and yearning to be with us. You are going to have choices about where you wish to go after your ascension. Some are ready to graduate to Arcturus, which is a very desirable entry point for you. Arcturus is a gateway to the galactic star systems of higher energy formations. As we have said before, beings who wish to graduate and move on to other parts of the galactic system must pass through our stargate. We are pleased to say that we are preparing some of you to come to Arcturus on your next incarnation after the ascension.

We know how difficult it has been for you on your path to accept higher consciousness. So much of the third-dimensional plane can be considered part of a dense consciousness. There is so much contraction, including much violence and hatred. You must rise above that now, and acknowledge your starseed connection. You must acknowledge your universal consciousness and your innate ability to expand that consciousness. You must move with total confidence in preparation for the fifth dimension. It has been a long road, and we know it has not come easily. You have experienced many forms of persuasion. Now you are going to have to work with others and help persuade them.

The Power of Group Energy

We welcome your energies and your spirits into the realms of the Arcturian frequencies. Many of you have waited a long time to align your energies with us, and to be able to receive our energies at the same time. It is usually much more effective to work with your energies in a group format because of the overwhelming denseness and lower frequencies on the Earth. Working with others in a group will help you to raise your frequencies and your receptivity to a higher level, which will better enable you to interface with us.

The group process and group strength is a well-known phenomenon on the Earth. The power of a group increases dramatically when you increase its numbers. Even a small group can create a powerful energy. It goes without saying that the entire frequency of your planet needs to be raised. Within a group format of concentrated effort, we are able to accelerate the raising of your frequencies. Likewise, you will then be able to do the same around your living areas. Because of your raised frequency, your mere presence in a physical area will have a strong effect.

We have spoken to you often about the importance of group energy and the importance of people meeting in groups. You can be stimulated and activated by group interactions. It is true that many of you have come into this incarnation as a group, have attended group classes before, and will have the opportunity to ascend as a group. It is very possible that people who are part of a spiritual group will stay together in the ascension, and it is very likely that you will see each other again on the other side, in the fifth dimension. Coming together now in groups will provide a base, a foundation for your work in moving to the next realm.

We look with admiration at how people are forming groups as a way of not only enhancing themselves, but also as a way of changing the human race. Each individual in the group contributes to the purification of the group subconscious, and, eventually, the entire group consciousness of the planet. There are many starseeds and lightworkers that are connecting in different ways, doing love meditations, and meditations for the Earth. The Arcturian group activities are very powerful in that they are helping to bring many people to a point of transformation. We are pleased to be a part of your subconscious purification.

THE NUMBER FORTY

Numbers are very powerful in mathematics and in the galaxy. Certain combinations of numbers can help individuals move into a specific mental and spiritual state of preparedness. The number forty is a very powerful number. We can tell you that it is a universal number, a proven number, and we have chosen it carefully. It has not only been the source of powerful energy for us, but it can create a great spiritual power on the Earth at this time. Forty is a galactic power number, and you gain a form of spiritual protection from working with this number. Now, you wish to know why the number forty has this power?

Forty is a number that brings you out of the spiritual wilderness into a heightened state that allows you to transcend the third dimension. It is the key number of spiritual transformation on the third dimension. With the power of forty, you can ascend. It is a magnification number. We have asked for the formation of groups of forty, for we know this number has the special power to elevate you. Each of you may have restrictions of consciousness that can not be overcome by yourselves. But with the power of forty, you can merge your consciousness into the group. This is important for you. You are merging. It is not a merging where you are giving up your consciousness. You are bringing your consciousness into the group process.

We on the Arcturian energy system are very tied to the number forty. It is a powerful number for us, much as you would use the number seven. In our system, the number forty is a number of perfection and completion. In working with your groups, we are loaning you our power system and our thought patterns. When you merge your thought patterns into a group energy, you will be able to activate and accelerate your thinking. You will build within a group of forty what you would call a critical mass of spiritual energy.

THE GROUP OF FORTY CONCEPT

A group of forty is a unit of consciousness created to build up the necessary energy to ascend. Forty as a unit is important, because it provides the energy frequency and the energy acceleration needed to move into the fifth dimension. Clearly, it will require a great deal of energy for you to move into the fifth dimension.

Imagine, if you will, that you must travel in a space ship to a distant star. In order to get to that star, you must travel at the speed of light, or as close to the speed of light as you can. We know that a tremendous amount of energy is required to accelerate and to travel a great distance—energy that is still beyond the reach of your scientific community at this time (although they are not as far away from this accomplishment as you may think). Likewise, it requires a tremendous amount of spiritual energy to actually skip the fourth and go directly into the fifth dimension from the third.

It will be possible for a few special individuals to generate enough energy to ascend to the fifth dimension and the stargate without participating in a group energy. However, a group energy will be required for the great majority of starseeds and lightworkers. It would be extremely difficult to generate that kind of spiritual force by yourself. However, as a group of forty, you can!

Many people like the personal contact of a smaller group, and do not like to be part of a really large group. A group of forty is small enough so that you can get to know everyone intimately. With a smaller number of members in each group, you will be able to concentrate your efforts on specific projects and tasks. Even though problems inevitably arise within a group of forty human beings, it is well worth your coming together in this way. We ask you to accept this.

Participating in a group of forty does not preclude involvement in any other groups. It will not interfere in any way with any other group activities. Groups of forty are always associated with the ascended masters. Do not feel that you have to compromise your beliefs in any way. We are working with you to help you ascend to the fifth dimension. We are constantly in contact with Sananda-Jesus and other masters. We want to help you remember your previous incarnations, and we want to help stimulate your memories so that you can access higher knowledge already learned in other lifetimes.

We want you all to understand that you have several memory systems, not just the Earth memory system. You all are carrying at least two, and up to ten other memory systems with you, systems that are as elaborate as the memory you have on the Earth. These memory systems can be linked. You can activate these other memories and bring in information, but you must prepare your mental body for the influx of higher energy and higher knowledge that will come in.

The years to come will be difficult years for the planet. They will be difficult for many reasons, and your commitment to a group process will serve you well during this time. It will provide a source of stability, a foundation for you. You will want to be able to slip in and out of the planet and the energy system that is holding you there. You will want to experiment, and experience being a lightbody that can move through the corridors, out of the Earth system.

You will need a focus, a place to go and persons to meet. It can be scary and confusing to leave the Earth plane, even temporarily, without some type of attachment, or grounding point. The Arcturians are available to help you work in these corridors, and move in and out of the Earth energy space. We are particularly trained to assist you in this, for when you are moving out of the energy field of the Earth, we will assist you in your detachments.

More explanation about the number forty needs to be addressed again. The number forty occurs on both sides—forty human beings on Earth and forty Arcturians on our ship. An Arcturian spiritual guide is assigned to work with every human being in a group of forty. Focus and connect with your Arcturian spiritual guide. Let yourself walk in their consciousness. They are Arcturian trainees who are skilled in allowing you to be in their consciousness and in their bodies. It is not just a one-way street. That is a common myth and error. It is a two way street. You can "walk-in" to an Arcturian! Does this not make sense? We are so highly trained and advanced, why could we not let your consciousness come into us? That is actually a more powerful connection. When you are in our consciousness, we can work with you on a much closer basis.

We have brought interdimensional ships into the Earth realm. On the ships, we have many Arcturians in deep meditation. These meditation groups on our ships are watching over the group of forty members on Earth. They are connecting with you telepathically and are sending you energy. We bring this powerful focus to you, and have created an actual energy bridge of which you are a part.

FORTY GROUPS OF FORTY

The group of forty membership will spread throughout the country and the world, and forty groups of forty will be created. After all the groups of forty are formed, there will be an increase in the dispersion of the Arcturian energy. Phenomenal numbers of people will want to come into these groups. The response will be overwhelming when this concept is announced and publicized. These initial forty groups, however, will not be the only ones who will work with the Arcturians. Others on the planet are already working very intensely with the Arcturian energy. But those of you who join the initial forty groups of forty will work with us in a special way, a way that is going to help us to manifest a planetary healing.

Our work with you is leading to a point that could result in a planetary intervention. Cosmic assistance, or a healing force, can be generated for the entire planet through our interactions with you. We are not here to rescue you, but to help you enhance, or amplify, your healing energies. You all need such a focus and direction. You now understand the necessity for an interactive network of groups, and how this interactive network will allow us to work with the Earth without incurring any negative karmic side effects. Most of all, you should understand how respectful we are to you and this planetary healing process.

The first groups of forty have already created a foundation for the other groups to come. The other groups may actually be more powerful and more closely connected with each other. It is always the founders, or beginners, however, that carry the burden, because they must lay the groundwork.

As we have said, forty groups of forty will form. At that point, you all are going to be steadily amplifying your energy. Each time another group of forty is formed, it bolsters the first group. The third group of forty bolsters the second and the first. The fourth group bolsters the third, second, and first. This is the power of forty. Do you understand this in terms of your factorial mathematics?

What is going to happen is that the forty groups of forty are going to be so powerful that one group will be able to ascend. When that one group ascends, thirty-nine groups will remain. Then, another fortieth group will form. Thus, the groups are going to move in and out. One group will ascend, and another group will form and take its place. This will be the group ascension pattern. We want to explain that there will also be other simultaneous ascension points, or waves. It is possible that all could ascend at a certain point. However, all of the forty groups will not go in the first wave. This is important: The groundwork for further ascensions must be carried on. As one group ascends, the responsibility for further group ascensions will be immediately transferred to the other groups.

It is not an effort for us to interact with you because you have heightened your energy so much. There is a stream of energy now that is coming through the current groups of forty. The initial groups are interacting, feeding on the group energy, and expanding. The channel is going to move into the next realm with the people in these groups. Many new people are coming in now, and each new member's subconscious is being cleansed. This happens automatically because the work of a group of forty becomes so powerful that it ultimately affects all of its members. People who are now joining new groups of forty, for example, are feeling the effect and power of the first two groups. Understand that the energy that is being generated is perceptible to others. This idea of purging the subconscious is going to be traveling through all the groups that will form.

MAINTAINING FIFTH-DIMENSIONAL CORRIDORS

The Earth is coming into its own as a place of spiritual upliftment. However, while many beings want to transform the Earth and be part of that process, there are beings who are working to prevent the planetary ascension. This is why we have called for the groups of forty to emerge as a powerful force to activate and anchor the energy necessary to insure that the Earth will complete its transformation.

The Native American Indians have predicted the possible collapse of the third dimension. Fifth-dimensional corridors must be maintained. We are talking about the planetary ascension now. Do not think for a moment that everything is going to open up instantaneously, and you are all going to go fifth-dimensional. Much preparation must be done now. This preparation is not only on a personal basis, but also on a planetary basis.

People will be "disappearing" up corridors in which you have been working. These corridors must be maintained on a regular basis. Just like a garden, if you do not maintain it by watering and weeding, the weeds will create rapid overgrowth. Even a powerful corridor, if surrounded by negative energies or forces, will close even in the presence of higher energy. Keeping the corridor open requires a steady exertion of higher energy. Imagine, with forty groups of forty members each, how many open corridors around the world there could be!

The groups of forty are going to be a pivotal influence on holding the connection to the fifth dimension. You may think that the fifth dimension is not connected to the Earth. The fifth dimension is indeed connected to the Earth. We alone are proof of that! Sananda-Jesus is also proof of that! Did he not come to your planet? The third dimension must be brought into order. Some of you will leave and not return to this dimension after the ascension. Nonetheless, the third dimension must be brought back into harmony. Bringing the third dimension into harmony can only be done with contacts such as this one.

GROUP OF FORTY LEADERSHIP AND FOCUS

A group leader does not have to be a channel, but he or she must be able to express the mission, carry on the mission, help organize and coordinate the efforts of the group, and insure the focus of the group. The leader's role is not to attract the members, that is the role of the channel. The leader of each group does not necessarily have to live in the area where the group forms.

Each group of forty needs a strong person to be the leader, as many group of forty members will be working on personal power issues. When the leader is not strong, the personal egos of the members become entangled, and can change the focus of the group. The focus of the group needs to be on entering the fifth dimension, establishing and maintaining corridors, personal healing and planetary grid work. A person who frequently connects with fifth-dimensional energy will emit a higher vibrational magnetic field. The leader's personal power can serve to amplify the connection the group has with us.

The most fundamental responsibility of each group is to maintain the focus of connecting to the fifth-dimensional energy. You can emit the magnetic energy that you are receiving from the fifth dimension. When you have a magnetic field of energy connected with the fifth dimension, then you will attract other starseeds. The magnetic energy field that you receive from the fifth dimension is a different vibration than any energy that you might receive from the third dimension. The first group of forty began by sending out thought waves through the fifth-dimensional corridors to other prospective group of forty members.

Part of your coming together in these groups has to do with fulfilling your mission as a starseed. Being in a group of forty will be a stepping stone that will lead to many other spiritual opportunities. The Arcturian groups of forty will become the central clearinghouse for all Arcturian information. They will become the central pivotal point for all of the Arcturian energy on the planet Earth. The interaction of the first group and the other groups of forty will become very powerful. Do not underestimate the power of these groups. The commitment of the people joining these groups now is far beyond what most others have had who have previously worked with the Arcturian energy.

THE ARCTURIANS WILL APPEAR

A time will come when all forty groups are going to meet simultaneously. This will be one of the first agendas after all forty of the groups of forty are established. There will indeed be a large congregation of Arcturian starseeds. You are going to lay the groundwork for an interdimensional interface. You are going to prepare a way for us to appear interdimensionally.

You have heard before that extraterrestrials who appear in the third dimension have the potential to take on karmic ties, or burdens, with the Earthlings. However, with the formation of the groups of forty, and with your meditations and interconnections, our appearing in your dimensional space will not be misconstrued. We will not be adversely affected by the laws of karma.

You will not in any way suffer from our coming into your space. We are very careful about these issues of karma and outside influences. We are also very respectful of your work and your free will. We feel that it is of utmost importance that all beings outside the third dimension respect and acknowledge your free will, as well as work with you in a way that you can comfortably interface with them. In this manner, there will be total evolutionary freedom.

The groups of forty provide that framework of freedom and karmic non-interference for all of you that are involved. Thus, it will be easier for us to appear to you. You will be able to assimilate this encounter without being traumatized or thrown off balance. With the preparation that we are providing, such an encounter will not dramatically change your life. You are evolving with us because you are interfacing and interacting with the fifth dimension. At the point of an appearance by us, you will be able to easily take it in stride.

One of the reasons why the extraterrestrials you call the Grays have discontinued their involvement in your planet and left the Earth is because they have begun to suffer from a karmic sickness. All who have interfered in a dramatic way with Earth's evolution have, in some way, experienced a karmic payback. It is usually a quick payback. It is not like your Earth experience, where you might have to wait three or four lifetimes in order to incur the negative results of your karma.

Currently, there is a form of protection around the Earth to prevent major interference from extraterrestrials. Other extraterrestrials have been able to interfere in the past. However, those who have done so with negative intentions have paid for the interference in some way. Those who come here to interact with Earth must now use a positive approach, similar to that which we are using, in order to avoid harmful karmic effects.

THE FLOW OF PROSPECTIVE ASCENDED MASTERS

The formation of the forty groups of forty establishes a pattern, or flow, of prospective ascended masters to enter the stargate. It is a group connection that will be impervious to all negative energies and to all assaults on the dimensional framework of the Earth. The mission of the forty groups is to prepare for ascension and to establish a consistent support for the third dimension by assisting in planetary electromagnetic grid work and the creation and maintenance of interdimensional corridors.

Different organizations of forty groups will emerge. The first forty groups will emerge based on the work of this channel. Others will also establish forty groups of forty originating from a central channel. This is a mission of awakening to the transformation into the stargate. One needs the mental clarity, which encompasses the knowledge of the stargate, before one can be totally transformed and go through it. The group of forty is the primary method we are using now. We have others who are also working with us.

We are convinced that working with groups of forty is the most direct, personal, and powerful way to assist you. We want to emphasize the word personal, because we are very much interested in each of you personally and the personal challenges that you face. We are interested in helping in you do whatever it takes to accelerate your growth. Thus, we are not interested in working with a thousand people at once, but rather in working with smaller groups. We are demonstrating our personal involvement with you. We send down the silver-gray light into your pineal gland. Let that point in your pineal gland be an access for higher mental clarity. I am Juliano. We are the Arcturians.

CHAPTER 16

THE SACRED TRIANGLE

We would like to speak to you about a triangle that has to do with the extraterrestrials, the White Brotherhood/Sisterhood, and the Native American Indians. This Sacred Triangle will assist the healing that needs to be completed on the Earth. It will help to move the Earth into the next dimension and thus benefit both the planet and all of humanity. The mission that you are on promotes this triangle and ensures that those with whom you come in contact will understand the vital link between these three aspects that forms what we choose to call the Sacred Triangle.

You will see that three forces are representative of the unifying force of the fifth dimension. You will note that an insignia of the triangle is on our clothes. The insignia contains a triangle with a circle of a planetary object over the triangle. In your three dimensions, you can not see through the planetary object, so you may have difficulty visualizing this. You have no way of drawing an object in which you can see through. However, this will be consistent with what you call a holographic artifact or holographic symbol.

It would be wonderful to have a recognizable symbol for this mission. We would like this symbol drawn so that it would be easily recognizable by all starseeds and lightworkers. This symbol would reflect all of these ideas that we are discussing. The symbol of the Sacred Triangle should be drawn interacting with a planetary object in the fifth dimension. You could use colors to represent the three sides, such as red for the Native American, white for the White Brotherhood/ Sisterhood, and blue for the extraterrestrials.

The Sacred Triangle represents three forces that must come together for a planetary healing to occur. Such healings have occurred on other planetary systems that we have worked with. The names White Brotherhood/Sisterhood, Native American, and extraterrestrial are representative of each aspect of that force within the triangle. Each force is bringing together a powerful energy. The Sacred Triangle is an image that represents a transformation and a unification. Your role is to activate people toward this understanding.

SIDE ONE: THE EXTRATERRESTRIALS

The first side represents the higher extraterrestrial forces that are currently working with the planet to bring to you the knowledge and the experience of the higher dimensions, and to explain the process of ascension. Secondly, the Arcturians and other higher extraterrestrial beings are maintaining many corridors connecting the third and fifth dimensions. These corridors are being used to pour fifth-dimensional energy into the Earth, allowing the planet to manifest its fifth-dimensional aspect. The corridors are also necessary for all human ascension into the fifth dimension.

In order for the ascension to occur, and in order for you to go through the ascension, you need to have an understanding of the fifth dimension. You need to understand that the fifth dimension exists, and that there are ways to currently access this dimension. You also need to understand that higher extraterrestrial beings reside in the fifth dimension, such as ourselves. We have come to teach you about the fifth dimension. We come to teach you in a way that will allow many of you to be spiritual activators for many others in the world.

We want to speak again about the Arcturian stargate, for that is the symbol on the extraterrestrial side of the Sacred Triangle. The stargate will soon be a force on this planet. We have helped to introduce the stargate, and the Arcturian stargate is now going to come into the consciousness of many people on the Earth. Just that consciousness alone is going to be transformational for thousands of people. Why? Think about this: You can go to a place where you can bring your past incarnations into a clear focus, and then proceed to direct your own future incarnations.

The stargate is the epitome of incarnation, because the pinnacle of the incarnational cycle is your ability to choose where you want to go. We know that you have been told on Earth that you have chosen your life conditions, but you have been strongly influenced by the divine guidance and wisdom of your spiritual masters and teachers. We are talking now about total independence in the choice of your evolutionary path.

You might say: "What if I am not ready to go to the stargate?" Know that you are going to go somewhere, I guarantee you. Because you are on this planet, you are not going to have a choice of staying and doing nothing. If you stay and go with the flow, the flow may bring you into darkness. Many people are not going to make it to the higher planes. If you do not choose, then you will just go with the masses who will start the incarnational cycle all over again on another third-dimensional planet. You have done that before!

We are on a mission of service. Our helping you to complete your Sacred Triangle is part of a higher triangle that we are working with. This will complete a triangle of service for us. Just as you are completing a triangle to move your consciousness and the planet to a higher dimension, we are completing a triangle that will move us to another realm, and bring us into a higher state of consciousness. Part of one side of our triangle is to be of service to you and others in your situation. This is the way the universe works. We exhibit our advancement by demonstrating and instructing you on Earth. From our view, what we do for you is done totally as a selfless act. We are doing this to complete our own mission. We do not look for personal gain from your planetary advancement.

The extraterrestrial energy, especially the Arcturian and Pleiadian energy, is bringing down to Earth the code for opening the corridors to the fifth dimension. This is the saving of the Earth that we are talking about. This is the saving of your biosphere. The fifth-dimensional light will be focused and directed toward the transformation of the Earth. The Arcturian Crystal Temple continuously radiates fifth-dimensional light back down through the Earth corridors. The constant flow of energy from the temple is essential to maintain these interdimensional corridors.

SIDE TWO: THE WHITE BROTHERHOOD/SISTERHOOD

The second side of the triangle represents the White Brotherhood/ Sisterhood, which is overseen by the Galactic Council. White refers to the spiritual color of pure light, and does not relate to race. Brotherhood/ Sisterhood does not relate to gender, but only to the name of a unified organization of ascended masters. The White Brotherhood/Sisterhood has been given the responsibility of working with the masses through the traditional religions, the angelic kingdom, and through other aspects of the white light.

This aspect of the triangle involves the energy of Sananda, Kuthumi, and other members of the White Brotherhood/Sisterhood working with the Earth. These ascended masters are responsible for maintaining all of the world's traditional religions. Through these religions, the masters have been helping you develop your spiritual I AM presence and your abilities to link to the Oneness of the Creator. The Creator Oneness energy is very strong in the higher dimensions. Overcoming the duality of the third-dimensional plane will allow you to experience that pervasive Creator energy.

The White Brotherhood/Sisterhood has been very active in helping certain powerful beings, such as Sananda-Jesus, Buddha, Mohammed, and others, to be divine forces and divine energies upon your planet. Each of these beings is a strong energy force for the Earth. Each can pull many millions of souls with them. It is known that a certain message, or way, must be given to bring many souls to a higher level. Many people on this planet follow traditional religions, and possess a very narrow and rigid understanding of the nature of the universe. These people can still move to the higher realms. It is the responsibility of a master teacher, such as Sananda-Jesus or Buddha, to bring their people to a higher place. From that place, they can be instructed to do what is necessary to move into the higher realms.

SIDE THREE: THE NATIVE AMERICANS

The final side of the triangle is the Native Americans. When we say "Native American," we do not just refer to the Native Americans on the continent of North America, but to indigenous, native peoples all over the world. It is their intimate knowledge of the Earth and the forces and dynamics of the Earth that help them to sustain the third dimension. A primary concept of the unification is to understand that while you are on the Earth, you are constantly interacting with the energy from the Earth. This is the Native American aspect, the sacred connection to Mother Earth.

The Native American ascended masters are working on a special planetary assignment. While their mission is moving to completion on Earth, they are also developing a parallel planetary experience for the Native Americans where they will be totally in control of their destiny again. There will be much celebration with the success of that mission.

The Native American energies have been in contact with the light from the galactic Central Sun. They hold a powerful light that has been given to them. Special frequencies have been given to certain native groups. These special frequencies enable the whole Earth dimension to remain intact. It is true that these certain vibrations and codes have to do with stabilizing the entire third dimension. These frequencies are so powerful that they come from the galactic center, the galactic core itself.

The Native American Indians, especially some of the Hopis, have been entrusted with certain codes that they are protecting to insure the survival of Mother Earth. The codes insure that the Earth does not return to a negative or out-of-control state. But it is now beyond their current abilities to fully protect these codes. They cannot now protect all of the Earth with their spiritual wisdom. They need the other parts of the code.

We know the nuclear energy that you use on Earth can totally upset these special codes and frequencies. Unknown to those who use nuclear energy is the fact that the entire dimension can be destroyed by certain mistakes. It was because of these things that our interventions, and the interventions of others, were ordered from the galactic center. Our interventions would insure that the codes and frequencies would not be destroyed. We are now spreading to many other lightworkers the knowledge of these frequencies that are so critical to the stabilization of the Earth dimension. The Native Americans who have these codes are not able to carry the burden by themselves. Therefore, lightworkers, know that you must also be carriers of this light-frequency vibration.

The Native Americans must be brought into an understanding that they are part of the triangle. They cannot continue to do their work alone. In the same way, the Sacred Triangle cannot be completed without them. Each side needs the other side (that is, on the Earth plane). How this message will be carried to the Native Americans, how they will react, and whether they will agree to participate, remains to be seen. There are many that are deeply involved in working with the Native Americans that have access to the powers held by their cultures.

JOINING THE SIDES OF THE TRIANGLE

We are the Arcturians, and I am Tomar. It has been part of the Arcturian mission to introduce the concept of the Sacred Triangle, and to oversee its development. It is a necessary unification of energy. Each aspect of this energy is very important. Some of you are familiar with all three energies. You are comfortable with the Native American energy, comfortable with the White Brotherhood/Sisterhood energy, and you are comfortable with the Arcturian and the extraterrestrial energy. A point in the center of the triangle unifies all three of these energies. It is possible to personally experience the unification of all three energies.

The earlier, so-called primitive people like the Native Americans did not have industrial technology, but the advanced ones possessed great spiritual technology. This is greatly admired by the Arcturians. They admire the Native American technology of spirit. It is a true creative manifestation from this Earth. We encourage you to use that spiritual technology and integrate it with the Arcturian spiritual technology and the spiritual technology from the White Brotherhood/ Sisterhood. Each has a unique aspect to offer. These are the energies that must be unified for the Earth to ascend

There are going to be those who can accept the Native American and the White Brotherhood/Sisterhood, but not the extraterrestrial. They will not be able to accept the stargate energy. How are those people going to be brought to understand the energy of the stargate, the energy of the Arcturians? On the other hand, those who are open to the extraterrestrial energies usually are very open to the other two. You may have problems with some people not immediately accepting the extraterrestrials. Others may not readily accept the spiritual energy of the Native Americans.

Some people will be working on different sides of the triangle. A person can be working only on one side and still be in alignment. For example, one who works only with the side of Sananda and the angelic hosts can still be in alignment, because they are carrying the energy of that side. The chosen or special ones are going to work toward the unification of all three sides. It will not take a large group of people to accomplish this unification.

I want you to focus on three very sacred places—two on the Earth, and one on Arcturus. The first place is the San Francisco Peaks next to Flagstaff, which will represent the Native American holy lands.

The second place is Mount Shasta in northern California, which will represent the energy and the presence of the White Brotherhood/Sisterhood. The third place is the Crystal Temple on Arcturus, which carries the Arcturian fifth-dimensional frequency.

I ask you now with me to go to all sides of the Sacred Triangle. First go to the San Francisco Peaks. From the Peaks, go to the crystal temple on Arcturus. Then travel from the crystal temple to Mount Shasta. Come back from Mount Shasta to the San Francisco Peaks, and complete the triangle. Now hold this triangle energy, and visualize the spiritual unification of the Earth. Now I ask you to visualize those three areas again, one by one, as you receive messages from beings at each location.

THE SAN FRANCISCO PEAKS

Let us first go the San Francisco Peaks, near the town of Flagstaff, Arizona. This is a high range that overlooks much of Arizona. It is a very holy area. Many Indian spirits reside there, but beings from the extraterrestrial realm also can be found. Feel the purity of light in this place. With your etheric body, leave a signature of your energy there.

This is Chief Buffalo Heart. I am proud to walk on the mountains of Saint Francis, the San Francisco Peaks. What a beautiful unification, San Francisco, Saint Francis, an aspect of Kuthumi. It has been written that when the white man returns to the teachings of the natives, then it will be time for the Earth to be healed. I know that many of you are ready to honor these teachings, and to honor the ascended masters of the Native Americans. I am here to tell you that the Native American ascended masters belong to all of you. We are open to working with all people who are of the Buffalo Heart.

The Buffalo Heart is a heart that is open to the animal world. It is open to the power animals. We know that the animals need the Earth. The animals cannot live unless their environment is pure, unless they are able to live in the laws of nature. The Buffalo Heart acknowledges that. The White Buffalo has returned to the plains. The White Buffalo is walking among you now in spirit and in actual physical manifestation. This is a symbol of the great unification and the work that will now be done.

The White Buffalo is a sign, but not the final one. This sign signifies that there will be forgiveness and a new era of understanding between the natives and the whites on this planet. This spirit of understanding began several years ago in 1987 with the Harmonic Convergence, and our working together has now intensified. The Sacred Triangle project acknowledges the need for unification and forgiveness. We, of the ascended masters, will be working with the Native Americans to help them understand that your intentions are pure, that you want to integrate the Sacred Triangle energies, and that they need your help.

The Native Americans cannot complete their tasks of healing the Earth and preserving this third dimension without you. We are working with them to overcome their paranoia and distrust of white people. We deeply understand their feelings, and why they do not want to share their spiritual knowledge with you. However, because time is short, all could perish if they hold the spiritual knowledge within and choose not share it. I have called on all of the Native American ascended masters to be with us. We will work to bring the energy of the Native Americans to this project, and the energy of the power animals as well.

Know that most of the ascended masters from the Native Americans have chosen to be of assistance to the Earth. Many more Native American spirits on the Earth are waiting to assist. We do understand that other native, indigenous cultures exist besides the Native Americans. However, the original call came from the Native Americans on this continent because of the special codes they carry. The Hopi carry a special knowledge of the third dimension and of the restoration of the spirit energy of this realm.

Greetings, brothers and sisters. I am Chief White Eagle, and I bless each and every one of you. I present you with the etheric eagle feather to guide you during this intense period at hand. I know that many of you wish to go into your awaiting lightbodies on the fifth dimension. However, we have a need for you to maintain your energy and your presence here on Earth. Look into your hearts, and see how many people you are now touching, and how many more you will touch in the near future. See how many people are going to come together through your efforts.

Many types of corridors, or places of high energy, still remain throughout the native lands. However, they have been partly closed, and are guarded by protective spirits. Therefore, special permission is needed to gain entry to these areas. A new kind of intersecting corridor is currently needed. The energy work connected with the Sacred Triangle can help to lay an important foundation for the creation of these corridors to the fifth dimension.

Because the Earth knows about the fifth dimension, she has served many people before you by enabling them to reach this higher level. If the Earth is addressed properly, the energy will open up for you. I speak now to Mother Earth. Blessed are you, Mother Earth. We live in joy upon the surface of your body. You are our Mother, as well as the mother of many other spirits. We accept our role as the guardian of your spiritual light. We send healings to you throughout the whole surface and throughout all of your oceans, skies, great rivers, and streams.

I speak to you tonight of the holy ceremony that must take place to prepare for the ascension of the Earth. A universal energy exists throughout the planet. This Earth life force permeates everything on the planet. You are part of that Earth energy. We must go within Earth, within her spirit, and tell her that we are ready to bring forth her beautiful light. To help her do this, we must direct a fifth-dimensional light into the Earth with a strong force. Then we will offer special prayers, special words spoken that will help to raise the Earth consciousness.

My friends, the Earth has been blunted. Her spiritual life has been clogged by what has been happening on the planet during the past two thousand years, but especially by the activities occurring during the past two hundred years. Many lightworkers have gone to different parts of the planet and have opened up energies and vortices. This evening we must go within Mother Earth. Travel with me this evening to the center of the spirit of Mother Earth.

From where you are sitting, descend into the Earth. Descend into her energy field as an energy being. Merge your body into the energy of the Earth, and speak these words: "Mother Earth, we come here to bring you into the fifth dimension. Mother Earth, we bring the light of the Arcturians into your spiritual realm. Mother Earth, we love you, and we commit ourselves to unlocking your ascension codes so that you may move forward." This is the purpose of the Native American ceremonies: the guarding, the unlocking, and the activating of the Mother Earth sacred codes.

I am very pleased that you are ready to include our wisdom and our teachings into the Sacred Triangle. I am pleased that so many of you are acknowledging the sacredness of the Earth. It is a sacred planet and a holy place. There are still many, many holy places on this planet. Holy places need to be nurtured and activated. From the highest points in the mountains, we can oversee what is taking place throughout the Earth. Much is happening that is destructive to the Earth and its people, and these things have been going on for centuries. But now, beautiful people like yourselves are carrying the torch of light for the planet. I smoke the peace pipe with you. This is White Eagle.

THE ARCTURIAN CRYSTAL TEMPLE

This is Tomar. Now I ask you to go to the crystal temple in your etheric body. Focus your third eye into the huge crystal. Establish a light frequency from the crystal to your third eye, and feel the energy coming into your third eye. Knowledge will come to you about how to assist in this unification. Leave a part of yourself here in the crystal temple. You now have two parts of yourself in two different sacred places.

This is Helio-ah, and we are the Arcturians. I am speaking to you from the Arcturian crystal temple. We are closely observing your changing energy patterns, and we are watching as you begin to integrate the Sacred Triangle energies. One of our roles is to offer you a group consciousness that will be pure. Also, another role is to attract many of the Arcturian starseeds to this Sacred Triangle project. The Arcturian starseeds were instrumental in beginning this project, and will be instrumental in completing this project. We who are calling and activating the starseeds want to awaken within them their role in unifying the third dimension with the fifth-dimensional light. This is one of the major responsibilities of the groups of forty.

It is only with fifth-dimensional light that the people of Earth are going to accept forgiveness, accept the unification, and transcend the negativity on the planet. The fifth-dimensional light from the crystal temple is a light of transcendence. It is a light that transcends the ego, a light of pure thought and a light of purification. When you understand the fifth dimension through the Arcturian frequencies, you will understand how to overcome duality. It is a place of powerful attraction of energy that is in harmony with the Creator Spirit.

The Native Americans you work with must be introduced to the crystal temple and the corridors. You will find that they will be more receptive than you might think, because the Native Americans have been visited by extraterrestrial for many centuries. This is not a new experience for them. They will be very open to the Arcturian frequency.

We are assisting the Earth by establishing corridors from the crystal temple. These corridors are going to be placed in different spots. I want you to know that the crystal temple is always there for you to use as needed. If you are in a confusing situation and you do not know which way to turn, come to the crystal temple. Go into the crystal and feel the purity of the thoughts and the purity of the light. The understanding of your situation will become clear.

We are the Arcturians, and I am Juliano. It is an incredible time to be on the Earth. We are aware of the alignments that your solar system is experiencing with the galactic center, or the Galactic Central Sun. We are aware of the openings, the corridors, the interdimensional opportunities that are here now. It is truly astounding because it is an experience and an opening that only occurs at certain times in a planet's history.

This is a time of personal acceleration. A vast opportunity now exists to make personal leaps in your consciousness and your soul evolution. It is truly a moment that many of you have waited for a long time—to come and incarnate, knowing the infinite possibilities and the wonderful opportunity to experience the ascension, the opening into the next dimension.

As you know, your planet currently has developed fascinating technology, but overall, you have not made similar spiritual progress as an entire planet. Your planetary system is in danger of collapse. It would only take one or two mad men to create total havoc. Your reality, your gasoline, your money, is but a flicker away from total destruction. In part, when we speak of the dangers of your dimension collapsing, we refer to these matters of banking, commerce, and oil. These are the factors that currently keep your third-dimensional reality alive. It is all so fragile.

Scientific technology by itself does not guarantee spiritual evolution. Yet, such a wonderful opportunity currently exists for spiritual evolution. We wonder why more people are not taking advantage of it. Never before on this planet has there been such a vast storehouse of knowledge unleashed. Never has there been so much interaction with extraterrestrials and other higher-consciousness beings. It is amazing to see the Earth from our perspective as we are coming in from the fifth dimension. Can you imagine seeing these wonderful beings of light around the Earth?

The more we can help you connect to the fifth dimension, the more unification can occur. The more that unification occurs, the more light comes to your planet, and the more you are participating in assisting aspects of the planet to ascend. Each of you here is responsible for a personal vibration of the planet that you are resonating with, an aspect of that reality that you are going to help to unify. You do not know the powers that are within this project. Many people on this planet are going to be doing similar tasks. You will be participating with others for the manifestation of planetary and dimensional unification.

Sananda-Jesus was so powerful when he was on this planet because he was living unification. He was walking on the planet as a unified being, assimilating the third and fifth dimension. You can do the same. You do not have to be the great healer, you do not have to sacrifice your life, you do not have to speak to the masses, and you do not have to turn water into wine. That was the role of Sananda-Jesus. Your role is to live the unification, to walk the unification for others to witness.

We Arcturians love our work with the Earth. We feel this is a holy task, a task of joy to bring spiritual technology to you. We know you want to enter the fifth dimension. One of the ways of increasing your frequency and accelerating your energy is to connect with the crystal temple. When you connect your energy here, you are going to vibrate at a faster and faster rate. We have a special place in the crystal temple that has been established for your linkage and your work. The crystal chamber holds special vibrations suited for all who come to this interdimensional place on Arcturus. The crystal temple carries your specific light vibration and light code. We will hold your place and your energy here in the crystal temple. We will also send a healing ray of light with you as you travel back through the corridor to Mount Shasta.

Mount Shasta

This is Tomar. Now go to Mount Shasta in your etheric body. There is so much light there. Sananda, Kuthumi, Saint Germain, Mother Mary, Quan Yin, and many other great masters and teachers reside in this corridor of light called Mount Shasta. Leave a part of your etheric self there. Now you are at all three sacred places simultaneously, and you are still in your physical body as well.

Greetings, loved ones, this is Mother Mary. The unification of the Sacred Triangle energies is a fulfillment of a mission that was started two thousand years ago. It is a mission that has to do with the planetary alignment, and has to do with opening to the energy that has been called the Savior energy. During his Earth mission, Jesus predicted that a time of great light and great resonance would be coming. First, however, a cleansing and a purification would have to occur.

If you stay on the path, remain in the higher light frequencies, understand and read the signs of the times and be in alignment with Sananda-Jesus and the ascended masters, you will be able to withstand the purification. You will be able to move into the new world to come, the fifth dimension.

I, Mary, have many friends among you. I know that many of you are filled with a love for the Earth. I know that you want to assist. This is what is so beautiful about you; you are truly eager to serve. What a blessing it is, working with you who want to serve. By serving, you are transcending your own ego. I know that you have many different concerns regarding your own individual karma, your development, your livelihoods, and your families. But you still have a sense of responsibility for the planet and for what is now transpiring. You want to help others, and you want to heal others.

I was so moved when I heard how many of you wished to be healers and that you are manifesting your healing light and healing energy. Our master Sananda-Jesus was the perfect example of healing—those who came into his energy field were instantly healed. I want those of you who are going to be healers to know that it is your energy field that will be the healing force. Those who come into your energy field will feel a strong awakening.

Working on the unification energy will help to stabilize the planet and help to stabilize you during the coming Earth changes. The importance of this aspect of the Sacred Triangle is our great love for you and the Earth, the fulfillment of the mission set forth by Sananda-Jesus, as well as the announcement and progression of the ascension, and bringing those of higher light into the fifth dimension. We, in the White Brotherhood/Sisterhood, are all committed to these tasks. We are committed to working with you through all your guides and teachers. Let the songs of the angelic presence reach your etheric ears. May the light from all of us touch your hearts.

This is Kuthumi. I am here in I AM presence. I am here to bring you the violet flame, and to insure that it stays within your energy field. It is a special service to reach out and unify the energies of the Sacred Triangle. The group of forty members are going to be reaching and teaching many people. In the teaching of unity, forgiveness must play an integral part. My message to you is that it is time to teach forgiveness, which is such a powerful healing energy. I cannot list the countless injustices and the pain and sorrow that have been inflicted upon so many people on this Earth. But we can manifest forgiveness, and heal the wounds of the past. One of the roles of the Sacred Triangle is to recognize that the Native Americans carry an important part in the preservation of the Earth and third dimension. Earth is destined to enter the fifth-dimensional realm by accomplishing the unification of the three Sacred Triangle energies.

Dear ones, I am Quan Yin. I am here to teach about compassion and understanding. I am here to teach about forgiveness. We are enjoying these connections that you refer to as the Sacred Triangle. You really are the only people on the planet who are now living in this powerful connection. You have come here to learn about the proper use and expression of personal power.

Many people on the Earth want to understand and forgive. I can lead many of you to the light of understanding. In order to forgive, you must first understand. You are going to have to carry from the White Brotherhood/Sisterhood energy the understanding of what is happening on this planet. You must understand that we are moving toward the fifth dimension, and understand that there are access points to the higher planes. You must understand that the planetary ascension process has already begun both for you and the Mother Earth.

It is very important that you understand that the pain and suffering of the peoples of the Earth were a necessary part of the growth of the human race, and you must forgive all things. You must understand and feel the love that the guides and teachers have for you. Many of the masters, including myself, have lived many human lifetimes on the Earth, and we know what it is like. We know the many difficulties, but we also think that you are carrying on wonderfully. You are accepting this role, this task of unification.

I ask that the light of the Buddha shine down on all of you, and may the light of the Buddha be part of the Sacred Triangle. May you carry the knowledge of the Buddha in your hearts. May you carry the understanding of life that the Buddha has, and may you use that understanding as part of the healing that you can transfer to the world. The Buddha chose the path of remaining on the Earth just as the Native American masters have done. He chose to wait until all are ready to come, and the energy of the Buddha is in alignment with the Sunat Kumara energy of the Earth. No effort . . . effortless. Be . . . ing. These are the lessons of the Buddha. I send you my love, my dear ones, but I also want to send you my admiration for your work on the unification.

This is Tomar. We have completed the visitation of the three sacred places representing the energy of the Sacred Triangle. You can see in moving around the Sacred Triangle how powerful this energy is going to be. The importance of the interdimensional corridors maintained by the crystal temple must be brought to the attention of everyone. They will serve as beacons for the many groups of forty. I ask each of you to activate a corridor on the planet wherever you wish. You are not only serving this project, but you are demonstrating multidimensional existence by being in all three sacred places at the same time. Bring yourself back from all three places, back into your physical body. All three forces of the Sacred Triangle will now protect you. You can live the unification, and you can walk the unification now.

ACTIVATING THE ASCENSION CODES

The coming together of the three Sacred Triangle energies will unlock powerful ascension codes on the Earth. When you work with codes, sometimes it is like a puzzle, where each piece must be put in its proper place. Then, when all pieces have been fit together, a great door opens. When your level of consciousness reaches a certain vibration, an internal code opens, and you are then given the visions of Ezekiel, the visions of the stairways to the heavens. You are given the visions of the entrance to the stargate. You are given entrance to the interdimensional corridors.

You have within you the potential to awaken to your Arcturian mission, awaken to your Pleiadian past lives, and awaken to your Arcturian connections. This is all part of the codes that we are talking about. We are now preparing you to raise all of your vibrations so that you can receive and activate new coded energy within you. This will be a manifestation of the groups of forty. You can become a catalyst for opening up codes within your own mental, physical, emotional, and spiritual bodies.

When a code within you is ready to open, you will hear a certain tone, and you will suddenly experience a burst of energy within your being. As part of their mission, the Arcturian groups of forty will help to activate others so they can also receive the energy burst and experience the opening of the codes. Some of you have already had these openings. Once you have experienced the energy burst and the opening of a code, you will be able to receive specific instructions on what to do next. You have known about the example of Moses going up to Mount Sinai. He received a burst of energy, and the codes were opened for him. Moses was then given instructions on what messages to deliver to his people.

Many of you are totally open, and your codes have already been merged and integrated into your consciousness. We are always working on two levels. We are working on the level of your personal enlightenment, and we are working on the level of service to the Earth. Each of you involved in this project will bring to the Sacred Triangle a certain light energy. Some of you will bring the Native American energy, some the Pleiadian energy. Some will bring the Mother Mary energy, some will bring others. The force of the merging of these three energies is going to unlock deeper ascension codes within the Earth.

It is very important for you know that the potential exists for many catastrophes. Many events are going to occur that are related to the purification of the Earth. But within the Earth herself are sacred codes, codes that were used by higher extraterrestrial beings to bring life to the planet. These codes were used to create the biosphere of the Earth. The fact that she developed in a certain way is all contained in a structural format within the Earth's body.

The method and the energy to bring the Earth into the higher dimensions is already encoded within her. No matter what happens on the surface of the Earth, people of higher vibration can reach the codes within the Earth. Once fully activated, untold beauty and emerging of light from the Earth will flood the planet. A beautiful, healing, warm light will come out to the surface. People who experience this will be struck with a ray of godliness. It has been described as the returning to the Garden of Eden. Everyone will be in a state of heaven on Earth.

THE SACRED TRIANGLE

The image of the Sacred Triangle is a symbol for the coming together of three forces which will unite to heal our planet Earth and guide her in her transition to the fifth dimension.

Sananda-Jesus represents the White Brotherhood/Sisterhood. The extraterrestrial beings are represented by the image of the Arcturian stargate. The native peoples are represented by symbols from Native American spirituality: a peace pipe, the buffalo, and the eagle.

The image is an attempt at a holographic portrayal of the Earth with the Sacred Triangle superimposed upon it. The size of the triangle represents the progress of these three forces in unifying the spiritual energies of our planet. With more progress, the Earth will eventually be completely inside the Sacred Triangle.

Of the four images, this last one flowed out of me effortlessly. I felt the divine resonance and power of this unification energy and felt very blessed to be able to bring forth this image.

Gudrun Miller

SANANDA SPEAKS

This is Sananda. Dear ones, this is truly a sacred task and a sacred journey that you are continuing to embark upon. I know of your love for this path and this journey. It is now the time that all planetary unification must occur on the Earth.

The unification that the Arcturians have designated as the Sacred Triangle is a deep soul mission for you and for all of the guides and teachers working with you. This unification project that you are striving to accomplish is fulfilling a mission of yours and mine. The Sacred Triangle is the representation of the unification of the third dimension with the fifth dimension. For many of you, this is your chosen Earth mission of which you will contribute and experience. This Sacred Triangle mission is one in which you will have a part in creating by participating in all its diverse aspects.

It truly becomes exciting for all of us to meet and unify our forces. The spiritual technology that the Arcturians are offering will help to unify the planet. The *Kaballah* teaches that unification is the uniting of an energy from the upper world with the lower world. It also states that it is the mission of the lightworkers to complete that unification. Only you as the Adam Kadmon, the human race of Adam, can unify this energy.

We are always concerned about the fate of the Earth. You receive news information daily about one aspect of the planet that becomes destroyed, another species becoming extinct, another danger from an aberrant leader, or even potential danger from an asteroid. A supernatural energy will be needed to complete the evolution of the Earth into the next dimension.

We have placed the Sacred Triangle over your etheric bodies so that you will understand the mission and the tasks before you. Those who are to be activated will be attracted to you. They will understand the triangle of energy, and you will be able to join with them to bring about this most necessary task. We will work with anyone who chooses to participate in the unification of the three Sacred Triangle energies.

You are moving quickly. There are not many people on the planet that could work with all three sides of the Sacred Triangle. You may think that you are not developed enough or powerful enough, or not good enough to do this task of unifying the three different aspects of the Sacred Triangle. We ask you: Who else can do this now? Who else is willing to bring this knowledge of the unity of these three sides and spread it to others? It is not a matter of your skills or your fortune. It is a matter of whether you are open and sincere to this task. Look upon this work as a unification of utmost importance.

These special Sacred Triangle energies need to be unified to save the planet and the third dimension from imminent collapse. The level of this unification work carries with it a great sacredness. The point of unification will be complete when there is a simultaneous convergence of the three Sacred Triangle energies. This will open the doorway for your planetary ascension. When the Sacred Triangle codes are opened, the seals that keep you on the Earth will also be loosened, and you will begin to merge your consciousness more easily into other dimensions. This is what has been called the removal of the seals. It can only happen after you activate the ascension codes. At that point, you may choose where you wish to go, for your work on the Earth will be complete.

I bring down a golden ray of light from my heart chakra to yours. The will of the Creator will be expressed through the completion of the Sacred Triangle unification project. Once completed, the fifth-dimensional doorway will be opened to allow entrance and upliftment of your souls to join us there. I send blessings to all on the Earth. This is Sananda.

GLOSSARY

Adamic
A term used to describe Homo sapiens, or "Earth Humans." Man (Adam) is formed from the Earth.

Adam Kadmon
The Hebrew term for the primordial or first human. It is the prototype for the first being to emerge after the beginning of creation.

Andromeda
A large spiral galaxy 2.2 million light years from the Milky Way galaxy. The Andromeda galaxy is the largest member of our local galactic cluster. It is commonly referred to as our sister galaxy.

Andromedans
An advanced, higher dimensional race of beings from the Andromeda galaxy. A specific group of Andromedans are currently working with the Arcturians in their effort to facilitate the planetary ascension process of the Earth.

Archangel
The term designates the highest rank of angels in the angelic hierarchy. The *Kaballah* cites ten archangels. They are considered messengers bearing divine decrees.

Arcturus
The brightest star in the Herdsman constellation, also known as Bootes. This is one of the oldest recorded constellations. Arcturus is also the fourth brightest star seen from the Earth. It is a giant star, about twenty-five times the diameter of the sun and one hundred times as luminous. It is a relatively close neighbor of ours, approximately forty light years

from the Earth. High up in the sky in late spring and early summer, Arcturus is the first star you see after sunset. You can find Arcturus easily if you follow the Big Dipper's handle away from the bowl.

Ascension
A point of transformation reached through the integration of the physical, emotional, mental, and spiritual self. The unification of the bodies allows one to transcend the limits of the third dimension and move into a higher realm. It has been compared to what is called the Rapture in Christian theology. It has also been defined as a spiritual acceleration of consciousness which allows the soul to return to the higher realms, and thus is freed from the cycle of karma and rebirth.

Astral Plane
The non-physical level of reality considered to be where most humans go when they die.

Ashtar
The commander over a group of spiritual beings who are dedicated to helping the Earth ascend. The beings that Ashtar oversees exist primarily in the fifth dimension,. and come from many different extraterrestrial civilizations.

Chakras
Energy centers of the human body system. These centers provide the integration and transfer of energy between the spiritual, mental, emotional, and biological systems of the human body.

Central Sun
The center of any astronomical star system. All star clusters, nebulae, and galaxies contain a nucleus at their center. Even the grand universe itself has a Great Central Sun at the center of its structure. In most cases, a giant star exists at the center of all star systems. The Great Central Sun of the Milky Way galaxy provides life-giving energy to the entire galaxy.

Channeling

The process of entering a meditative trance in order to call forth other entities to speak through you.

Corridors

Transitional pathways on Earth that lead to a higher dimension. Corridors can be found in high-energy places such as sacred sites on the Earth. The Arcturians believe that we can establish corridors within our meditation areas on Earth.

Crestone, Colorado

A small town in Southeastern Colorado that has become a unique spiritual center. The Arcturians state that many corridors and energy centers exist in Crestone that link the area to key fifth-dimensional sites such as their home world, the Arcturian crystal temple, and the Arcturian stargate.

Crystal Temple

An etheric temple on the fifth dimension that has been made available for our use by the Arcturians. The crystal temple contains a lake over one mile in diameter which houses a huge crystal half the size of the lake itself. The entire lake and surrounding area is encompassed by a huge glass dome, allowing visitors to also view the stars.

Eck

Ascended masters who are adepts of Eckankar, the ancient science of soul travel.

Eckankar

The all-embracing life force. An ancient science, now practiced by followers of Eckankar, that teaches you how to free the soul from the body and accomplish soul travel. Eckankar followers believe that etheric masters and teachers exist whose primary task is to aide us in our evolutionary development.

Etheric

A term used to designate the higher, non-visible bodies in the human system. In India, etheric is used to describe the unseen energy and thoughts of humans.

Ehyeh

In Hebrew, the supreme name of God. This is the name for God given to Moses in Genesis 3:14. *Ehyeh Asher Ehyeh* is the full name translated as I AM THAT I AM.

Group of Forty

A concept of group consciousness suggested by the Arcturians for our use in the group ascension process. According to the Arcturians, forty is a spiritually powerful number. The Arcturians emphasize the value and power of joining together in groups. A group of forty consists of forty different members located throughout the U.S. and worldwide who focus on meditating together at a given time each month. Group interactions and yearly physical meetings are recommended. Members agree to assist each other in their spiritual development. The Arcturians have asked that forty groups of forty be organized. These groups will assist in the healing of the Earth and provide a foundation for individual members' ascension work.

HAARP

High Frequency Active Aural Research Project. A scientific research project conducted by the U.S. military that some have described as an aspect of the Star Wars project. High-frequency radio waves are sent into the ionosphere with the purpose of jamming all global communications systems. It is being tested in the remote bush country of Alaska. The project uses a radio transmitter of immense power. It offers a unique ionosphere heating capability.

Grays, or Greys

See the glossary entry for Zeta Reticuli.

Kaballah

The major branch of Jewish mysticism. The Hebrew word *Kaballah* is translated as "to receive."

Kadosh
Hebrew word for holy.

Kadosh, Kadosh, Kadosh, Adonai Tsevaot
Hebrew for "Holy, Holy, Holy is the Lord of Hosts." This is a powerful expressoin which, when toned, can raise one's level of consciousness to new heights and assist in unlocking the codes for our transformation into the fifth dimension.

Kuthumi
One of the ascended masters who serves Sananda. In a previous life, Kuthumi incarnated as Saint Francis of Assisi. He is generally recognized as holding the position of world teacher in the planetary White Brotherhood/Sisterhood.

Metatron
Tradition associates Metatron with Enoch who "walked with God" (Genesis 5:22) and who ascended to heaven and was changed from a human being into an angel. His name has been defined as the Angel of Presence, or the one who occupies the throne next to the divine throne. Another interpretation of his name is based on the Latin word metator, which means a guide or measurer. In the world of the Jewish mystic, Metatron holds the rank of the highest of the angels. According to the Arcturians, Metatron is associated with the stargate and is assisting souls in their ascension to higher worlds.

Michael
His name is actually a question, meaning: "Who is like God?" He is perhaps the best known of the archangels and is acknowledged by all three Western sacred traditions. He has been called the Prince of Light, fighting a war against the Sons of Darkness. In this role, he is depicted most often as winged, with unsheathed sword, the warrior of God and slayer of the Dragon. His role in the ascension is focused on helping us to cut the cords of attachment from the earth plane, which will allow us to move up to higher consciousness. In the *Kaballah*, he is regarded as the forerunner of the *Shekhinah*, the Divine Mother.

Monad

The original, elemental creative force. Each one of us contains a portion of that force at the center of our true essence.

Montezuma's Well

A tourist attraction in central Arizona near the Sedona area. Originally, historians mistakenly identified the deep well as belonging to the Aztec Indians from Mexico. Later, archaeological work identified the area as belonging to the Sinagua Indians, contemporaries of the Anasazi. The Arcturians identify this area as being a powerful corridor and a wonderful area for meditations and experiencing other dimensions.

Nephilim

Hebrew for "the fallen ones." This term is used in Genesis 6:4 in reference to the giants: "It was then, and later too, that the Nephilim appeared on Earth—when the divine beings cohabited with the daughters of men, who bore them offspring."

Null Zone

A zone outside of the third dimension, but not necessarily in any other dimension. An area outside of our known time-space universe structure where time is nonexistent. Some have speculated that the Photon Belt contains null-zone regions, and the Earth will temporarily enter a null zone in the near future.

Orion

Orion is a superb constellation that dominates the winter southern sky. The most striking part of the constellation is the belt, which consists of three bright stars. No other constellation contains so many bright stars. Rigel, which is outside the belt, for example, is a giant star over five hundred light years away. Betelgeuse, another star outside the belt in Orion, is about three hundred light years away.

Orions

An extraterrestrial culture that descended from another ancient civilization near the constellation Orion. The Orions have been extremely influential in the genetic makeup of the current human being. Human beings possess a portion of Orion DNA and reflect Orion traits in our current physical, emotional, and mental composition.

Photon Belt

An energy belt emanating from the center of the galaxy that is about to intersect with the solar system and the Earth. Some have predicted the Photon Belt contains energy particles that could affect the Earth's electromagnetic field, causing all electronic equipment to stop working.

Pleiades

A small cluster of stars known as the Seven Sisters in some mythologies. Some Native American Indians believe that they are descended from the Pleiades. It is near the constellation Taurus, around 450 light years from the Earth, and is the home of a human race called the Pleiadians, who have frequently interacted with the Earth and her cultures. It is said that the Pleiadians have a common ancestry with us.

Sananda

Sananda is the one who is known to us as the Master Jesus. He is considered the greatest Jewish Kaballist of all times. His galactic name— Sananda—represents an evolved and galactic picture of who he is in his entirety. In the *Kaballah*, Sananda is known as Jeshua ben Miriam of Nazareth, which can be translated as Jesus, son of Mary of Nazareth.

Sacred Triangle

A term used by the Arcturians to denote a triangular symbol representing the unification of three powerful, spiritual forces on Earth: the White Brotherhood/Sisterhood masters including Sananda-Jesus, the ET higher-dimensional masters such as the Arcturians and the Pleiadians, and the Native American Indian ascended masters such as Chief White Eagle. The unification of these spiritual forces will create the Sacred Triangle that will aid in the healing and the ascension of the planet Earth.

Stargate
A multidimensional portal into other higher realms. The Arcturian stargate is very close to the Arcturus star system, and it is overseen by the Arcturians. This powerful passage point requires that Earthlings who wish to pass through it must complete all lessons and Earth incarnations associated with the third-dimensional experience. It serves as a gateway to the fifth dimension. New soul assignments are given there, and souls can then be sent to many different higher realms throughout the galaxy and universe. Metatron and many other higher beings are present at the stargate. Many people are now using the term stargate to refer to openings on the Earth to higher dimensions, when in fact they are describing corridors. The stargate is a magnificent, temple-like, etheric structure that can process and transform many souls.

Tachyon
A small particle that travels faster than the speed of light. A tachyon stone is an object that contains tachyon particles and is used for healings in much the same way that one uses crystals.

Thought Projection
A technique described by the Arcturians involving projecting thoughts through a corridor to reach the fifth dimension and beyond.

Tones
Sounds that produce a vibratory resonance that helps to activate and align the chakras.

Walk-ins
Humans who have received other spiritual entities into their bodies. The term is also used in reference to the new spirit that has entered the body. In some cases the original spirit of the person may have left (for example, after an auto accident or some other form of severe trauma) and the new spirit "walks in" the old body.

White Brotherhood/Sisterhood

The White Brotherhood/Sisterhood is a spiritual hierarchy of ascended masters residing in the fifth dimension. White is not used here as a racial term. It refers to the white light or higher frequency that these masters have attained. The masters include Sananda, Kuthumi, Mother Mary, Quan Yin, Sanat Kumara, Saint Germain, and many, many other ascended beings.

Zeta Reticuli

A twin star system that is the home of small, humanoid beings with large, black oval eyes that have visited the Earth for over fifty years. They are often referred to as the Grays, or Zetas. They have been accused of abducting humans for DNA research and other medical experiments.

Zoharic Light

Light from the Creator source. *Zohar* is the Hebrew word for brilliance, or splendor.

DAVID K. MILLER

David K. Miller is the director and founder of an international meditation group focused on personal and planetary healing. He has been director of this global healing group, called the Group of Forty, for over fifteen years. Using group consciousness, David has been developing groundbreaking global healing techniques. In his way, he works to direct powerful healing group energy to help restore areas in the Earth that need balance, healing, and harmony. The technique he uses with his group work is called biorelativity, which uses group consciousness work to restore the Earth's "feedback loop system," a complex planetary system that maintains the correct balance of our planet's atmosphere, ocean currents, and weather patterns.

David's mediation group has over 1,200 members worldwide. In addition to his lectures and workshops, David is also a prolific author, with numerous books and articles on Earth healing techniques. His most recent books include *Teachings of the Sacred Triangle*, volumes 1 through 3, *New Spiritual Technology for the Fifth-Dimensional Earth*, and *Raising the Spiritual Light Quotient of the Earth*. Several of his books have also been published in German and Spanish.

David works together with his wife, Gudrun Miller, who is a psychotherapist and visionary artist. Together they have conducted workshops in Brazil, Germany, Australia, Mexico, Argentina, Costa Rico, Spain, New Zealand, Belgium, Turkey, and Spain. David's foundation for this work lies in his study and connection to Native American teachings and his intense study in mysticism, including the *Kaballah*. He also has an intense interest in astronomy and the relationship of the Earth to the galaxy.

GUDRUN MILLER

I have been an artist for twenty years and have been a spiritual seeker all of my life. When asked by the Arcturians to bring forth images with their assistance, I was honored and thrilled.

My spiritual awakening was assisted by my spirit guide, Spirit Fire, an ascended American Indian. She helped me build a medicine teepee in our back yard and has also guided me in my work as a visionary artist. Many people have since come from all over the world to experience the healing energies of the Eagle Medicine teepee. The American Indians worked in harmony with the extraterrestrial energies and the White Brotherhood/Sisterhood. I believe I am following an old tradition that seems entirely congruent with my personal quest.

The Arcturians make their requests through David, who then channels specific information that helps to stimulate my imagination. I then sense their presence in a heightened awareness and focus as I paint. The Arcturians have reassured me that if the images were not suitable, they would tell me. They have requested many more images that I have not painted yet, but I hope to in the near future.

When not painting, I work full time as an art therapist and counselor. I sense the healing presence of my guides and teachers in my practice as well.

♃ Light Technology PUBLISHING

the PRISM of LYRA

An Exploration of Human Galactic Heritage

Revised and Updated

the PRISM of LYRA
An Exploration of Human Galactic Heritage
Lyssa Royal • Keith Priest

This is an introductory book that examines the idea of creation in a different light. In contrast to the notion that humans are the result of creation, it explores the idea that the collective humanoid consciousness (or soul) created our universe for specific purposes.

What are those purposes? Who is involved? These questions and many more are addressed, resulting in startling possibilities.

The Prism of Lyra then traces various developing extraterrestrial races (such as those from the Pleiades, Sirius, and Orion) through their own evolution and ties them into the developing Earth. Highlighted is the realization of our galactic interconnectedness and our shared desire to return home.

$16$⁹⁵

Plus Shipping

ISBN 978-1-891824-87-6`
Softcover 176 PP.
6 x 9 Perfect Bound

PREPARING FOR CONTACT

A Metamorphosis of Consciousness

by Lyssa Royal and Keith Priest

ET contact is happening now. We may not remember it clearly. We may think it is only a dream. We may ignore the signs of ET contact simply because we do not understand them. And most of all, we may simply be too frightened to fully acknowledge its presence.

This ground-breaking book is a combination of narrative, precisely-focused channeled material from Lyssa and personal accounts. An inside look at the ET contact experience is given, including what the human consciousness experiences during contact with an extraterrestrial. How do our perceptions of reality change during contact? How can we learn to remember our contact experiences more clearly?

As you journey through the pages of this book you will also take an inner journey through your own psyche and discover a whole new dimension to your unexplained experiences. Join us on the path of transformation as humankind begins . . .

$16.$⁹⁵

ISBN 978-1-891824-90-6

Visit our online bookstore: www.LightTechnology.com

Shamanic Secrets Mastery Series
Speaks of Many Truths and Reveals the Mysteries through Robert Shapiro

Shamanic Secrets for Material Mastery

This book explores the heart and soul connection between humans and Mother Earth. Through that intimacy, miracles of healing and expanded awareness can flourish. To heal the planet and be healed as well, we can lovingly extend our energy selves out to the mountains and rivers and intimately bond with the Earth. Gestures and vision can activate our hearts to return us to a healthy, caring relationship with the land we live on. The character of some of Earth's most powerful features is explored and understood, with exercises given to connect us with those places. As we project our love and healing energy there, we help the Earth to heal from human destruction of the planet and its atmosphere. Dozens of photographs, maps and drawings assist the process in twenty-five chapters, which cover the Earth's more critical locations.

498 p. $19.95 ISBN 978-1-891824-12-8

Shamanic Secrets for Physical Mastery

Learn to understand the sacred nature of your own physical body and some of the magnificent gifts it offers you. When you work with your physical body in these new ways, you will discover not only its sacredness, but how it is compatible with Mother Earth, the animals, the plants, even the nearby planets, all of which you now recognize as being sacred in nature. It is important to feel the value of oneself physically before one can have any lasting physical impact on the world. If a physical energy does not feel good about itself, it will usually be resolved; other physical or spiritual energies will dissolve it because it is unnatural. The better you feel about your physical self when you do the work in the previous book as well as this one and the one to follow, the greater and more lasting will be the benevolent effect on your life, on the lives of those around you and ultimately on your planet and universe.

576 p. $25.00 ISBN 978-1-891824-29-5

Shamanic Secrets for Spiritual Mastery

Spiritual mastery encompasses many different means to assimilate and be assimilated by the wisdom, feelings, flow, warmth, function and application of all beings in your world that you will actually contact in some way. A lot of spiritual mastery has been covered in different bits and pieces throughout all the books we've done. My approach to spiritual mastery, though, will be as grounded as possible in things that people on Earth can use— but it won't include the broad spectrum of spiritual mastery, like levitation and invisibility. I'm trying to teach you things that you can actually use and benefit from. My life is basically going to represent your needs, and it gets out the secrets that have been held back in a storylike fashion, so that it is more interesting."

—Speaks of Many Truths through Robert Shapiro

768 p. $29.95 ISBN 978-1-891824-58-6

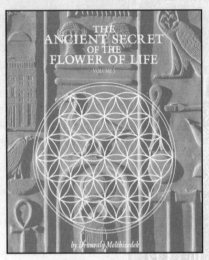

THE ANCIENT SECRET
OF THE FLOWER OF LIFE
VOLUME 2

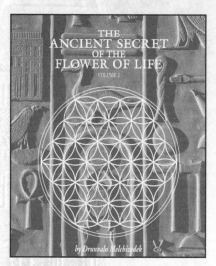

BEYOND THE LIGHT BARRIER
by Elizabeth Klarer

This autobiography of a South African woman is the story of the interstellar love affair between the author and Akon, an astrophysicist from the planet Meton in Alpha Centauri. Elizabeth Klarer travelled to Meton with Akon, lived there for four months with his family, and gave birth to his son. Featuring fascinating descriptions of the flora, fauna, and advanced technology of Akon's people, this classic is being reissued in a long-overdue new edition.

$15.⁹⁵

244 P. SOFTCOVER
ISBN 978-1-891824-77-7

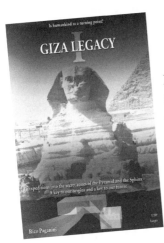

GIZA LEGACY I
by Rico Paganini

In this groundbreaking book, Rico Paganini provides a fascinating overview of developments and discoveries involving the pyramids and the Sphinx. Using modern technology combined with spiritual sensing abilities, he has discovered that the real secret of the pyramids was yet to be recognized. Both in and below the pyrmids lies the key to a liberating truth for all those who seek it.

$40.⁰⁰

250 P. HARDCOVER
60 MAPS; 250 COLOR PHOTOS
ISBN 978-3-9522849-0-2

⚜ *Light Technology* PUBLISHING

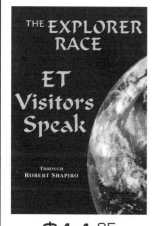

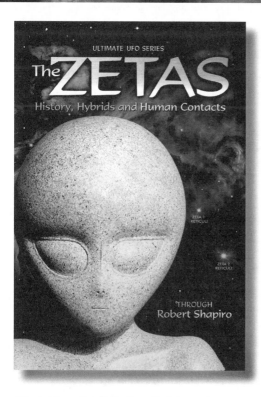

✦ *Light Technology* PUBLISHING

PLANT SOULS SPEAK
A NEW WAY OF INTERACTING WITH PLANTS

"What we intend to speak about—if I may speak in general for all plants—is how you can interact with plants in a more benevolent way for you as the human species. For a long time, you have been clear on medicinal uses of leaves and stems and seeds and flower petals and so on, but you are only getting about one-tenth of the energy available to you that way. It is always better to interact with the plant and its energies in its live form, but you need to know how.

"The intention of this book is to reveal that formula so that you can stop searching, as a human race, for the magical cures to diseases by exhausting the supply of life forms around you, when a much simpler process is available. This book will not just comment on things you know about but show you what you are missing in your interaction with plants."

—Dandelion

Chapters Include:

Cherry Tree	Maple Tree	Palm Tree	Peach Tree
Pine Tree	Redwood	Walnut Tree	Brown Rice
Crabgrass	Oat Grass	Wetland Grass	Angelica
Bamboo	Corn	Daffodil	Dandelion
Hibiscus	Holly	Ivy	Kelp
Marijuana	Orchid	Rose	Sage

$16.⁹⁵
ISBN 978-1-891824-74-6
Softcover, 286 pp.

ANIMAL SOULS SPEAK
THROUGH ROBERT SHAPIRO

Robert Shapiro is largely known as a professional trance channel, with several series of published books such as The Explorer Race Series, of which this is book #13; Shining the Light Series (8); Shamanic Secrets Series (3); Benevolent Magic, and the Ultimate UFO Series.

But, as he is now, he is a mystical man with shamanic capabilities well and thoroughly infused into him. He also has many unusual skills that he is teaching through blogs, the Sedona Journal of Emergence and these books. It is his intention to bring about the most benevolent change available on the planet through sharing his personal inspirations as well as his channeling, which in this book is of these wonderful beings humans call animals.

Chapters Include:

Eel	Tortoise	Frog	Skunk
Snail	Deer	Elephant	Rabbit
Polar Bear	Earthworm	Phoenix	Chickadee
Koala Bear	Spider	Cat	Dog
Whale	Shark	Gnat	Butterfly
Myna Bird	Llama	Sea Sand	Giraffe
Manta Ray	Ant		

$29.⁹⁵
ISBN 1-891824-50-3
Softcover, 640 pp.

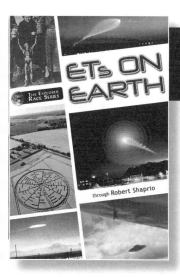

ETs ON EARTH
through **Robert Shaprio**

ETs on Earth:

- Blue Spiral Light over Norway
- Humans Are Going through Rapid Changes on Earth
- How You Traverse to Your Home Planet in Deep Sleep to Recharge
- Will There be a Phony ET Invasion on Earth?
- Beware of a Staged, Fake ET Invasion
- You Moved Earth Out of Phase to Test Your Creator Abilities. "Oops!" What You Can Do Now to Fix it.
- ETs Land in Soviet Union September 1989

- Brave ETs Who Stayed Behind So the Rest of Their People Could Go Home Are Captured
- ETs Visit with Russian Politician in Moscow
- ET Contact with the President of the Russian Republic of Kalmykia
- ET on the Ship That Created This Crop Circle
- ET from Ship Filmed Over Xiaoshan Airport, Hangzhou, China on 7 July 2010

$16⁹⁵
Plus Shipping
ISBN 978-1-891824-91-3
Softcover 435 pp.

TIME AND THE
TRANSITION TO NATURAL TIME

"The purpose of this book is to provide a context for your lives in the sequence you find yourselves in now. This explanation of time—and, to a degree, its variables—is being provided for you so that you will understand more about your true, natural, native personalities and so that you will be reminded that you are, as you know, in a school and that this school is purely temporary.

You don't come here very often to this place of linear time; like your own human lives, you are in school for only so long, and then you live your lives. When you exist beyond this school, you will find all those lives infinitely easier, and even as the Creator, your lives will be easier than they are in their single, linear lives that you're living now, because you will have all your components."

—Founder of Time

Chapters Include:
Time Is Now Available for Your Personal Flexibility
Your Blinders Are Coming Off
You Live in a Stream Hosted by Planet Earth
Time Is an Application for Expansion
Moving Toward Complete Safety and Benevolence
Transition to the Future in Warmth and Safety
The Gift of Time
Linking from Future Selves

$16.⁹⁵
ISBN 978-1-891824-85-2
Softcover, 286 pp.

⚱ *Light Technology* PUBLISHING

THE EXPLORER RACE SERIES

ZOOSH AND HIS FRIENDS THROUGH ROBERT SHAPIRO

THE SERIES: Humans—creators-in-training—have a purpose and destiny so heartwarmingly, profoundly glorious that it is almost unbelievable from our present dimensional perspective. Humans are great lightbeings from beyond this creation, gaining experience in dense physicality. This truth about the great human genetic experiment of the Explorer Race and the mechanics of creation is being revealed for the first time by Zoosh and his friends through superchannel Robert Shapiro. These books read like adventure stories as we follow the clues from this creation that we live in out to the Council of Creators and beyond.

❶ THE EXPLORER RACE

You individuals reading this are truly a result of the genetic experiment on Earth. You are beings who uphold the principles of the Explorer Race. The information in this book is designed to show you who you are and give you an evolutionary understanding of your past that will help you now. The key to empowerment in these days is to not know everything about your past, but to know what will help you now. Your number-one function right now is your status of Creator apprentice, which you have achieved through years and lifetimes of sweat. You are constantly being given responsibilities by the Creator that would normally be things that Creator would do. The responsibility and the destiny of the Explorer Race is not only to explore, but to create. 574 P. $25.00 ISBN 0-929385-38-1

❷ ETs and the EXPLORER RACE

In this book, Robert channels Joopah, a Zeta Reticulan now in the ninth dimension who continues the story of the great experiment—the Explorer Race—from the perspective of his civilization. The Zetas would have been humanity's future selves had not humanity re-created the past and changed the future. 237 P. $14.95 ISBN 0-929385-79-9

❸ EXPLORER RACE: ORIGINS and the NEXT 50 YEARS

This volume has so much information about who we are and where we came from—the source of male and female beings, the war of the sexes, the beginning of the linear mind, feelings, the origin of souls—it is a treasure trove. In addition, there is a section that relates to our near future—how the rise of global corporations and politics affects our future, how to use benevolent magic as a force of creation and how we will go out to the stars and affect other civilizations. Astounding information. 339 P. $14.95 ISBN 0-929385-95-0

❹ EXPLORER RACE: CREATORS and FRIENDS
The MECHANICS of CREATION

Now that you have a greater understanding of who you are in the larger sense, it is necessary to remind you of where you came from, the true magnificence of your being. You must understand that you are creators-in-training, and yet you were once a portion of Creator. One could certainly say, without being magnanimous, that you are still a portion of Creator, yet you are training for the individual responsibility of being a creator, to give your Creator a coffee break. This book will allow you to understand the vaster qualities and help you remember the nature of the desires that drive any creator, the responsibilities to which a creator must answer, the reaction a creator must have to consequences and the ultimate reward of any creator. 435 P. $19.95 ISBN 1-891824-01-5

❺ EXPLORER RACE: PARTICLE PERSONALITIES

All around you in every moment you are surrounded by the most magical and mystical beings. They are too small for you to see as single individuals, but in groups you know them as the physical matter of your daily life. Particles who might be considered either atoms or portions of atoms consciously view the vast spectrum of reality yet also have a sense of personal memory like your own linear memory. These particles remember where they have been and what they have done in their infinitely long lives. Some of the particles we hear from are Gold, Mountain Lion, Liquid Light, Uranium, the Great Pyramid's Capstone, This Orb's Boundary, Ice and Ninth-Dimensional Fire. 237 P. $14.95 ISBN 0-929385-97-7

❻ EXPLORER RACE and BEYOND

With a better idea of how creation works, we go back to the Creator's advisers and receive deeper and more profound explanations of the roots of the Explorer Race. The liquid Domain and the Double Diamond portal share lessons given to the roots on their way to meet the Creator of this universe, and finally the roots speak of their origins and their incomprehensibly long journey here. 360 P. $14.95 ISBN 1-891824-06-6

THE EXPLORER RACE SERIES

ZOOSH AND HIS FRIENDS THROUGH ROBERT SHAPIRO

❼ EXPLORER RACE: The COUNCIL of CREATORS

The thirteen core members of the Council of Creators discuss their adventures in coming to awareness of themselves and their journeys on the way to the Council on this level. They discuss the advice and oversight they offer to all creators, including the Creator of this local universe. These beings are wise, witty and joyous, and their stories of Love's Creation create an expansion of our concepts as we realize that we live in an expanded, multiple-level reality. 237 P. $14.95 ISBN 1-891824-13-9

❽ EXPLORER RACE and ISIS

This is an amazing book! It has priestess training, Shamanic training, Isis's adventures with Explorer Race beings—before Earth and on Earth—and an incredibly expanded explanation of the dynamics of the Explorer Race. Isis is the prototypal loving, nurturing, guiding feminine being, the focus of feminine energy. She has the ability to expand limited thinking without making people with limited beliefs feel uncomfortable. She is a fantastic storyteller, and all of her stories are teaching stories. If you care about who you are, why you are here, where you are going and what life is all about—pick up this book. You won't lay it down until you are through, and then you will want more. 317 P. $14.95 ISBN 1-891824-11-2

❾ EXPLORER RACE and JESUS

The core personality of that being known on the Earth as Jesus, along with his students and friends, describes with clarity and love his life and teaching two thousand years ago. He states that his teaching is for all people of all races in all countries. Jesus announces here for the first time that he and two others, Buddha and Mohammed, will return to Earth from their place of being in the near future, and a fourth being, a child already born now on Earth, will become a teacher and prepare humanity for their return. So heartwarming and interesting, you won't want to put it down. 354 P. $16.95 ISBN 1-891824-14-7

❿ EXPLORER RACE: Earth History and Lost Civilization

Speaks of Many Truths and Zoosh, through Robert Shapiro, explain that planet Earth, the only water planet in this solar system, is on loan from Sirius as a home and school for humanity, the Explorer Race. Earth's recorded history goes back only a few thousand years, its archaeological history a few thousand more. Now this book opens up as if a light was on in the darkness, and we see the incredible panorama of brave souls coming from other planets to settle on different parts of Earth. We watch the origins of tribal groups and the rise and fall of civilizations, and we can begin to understand the source of the wondrous diversity of plants, animals and humans that we enjoy here on beautiful Mother Earth. 310 P. $14.95 ISBN 1-891824-20-1

⓫ EXPLORER RACE: ET VISITORS SPEAK

Even as you are searching the sky for extraterrestrials and their spaceships, ETs are here on planet Earth—they are stranded, visiting, exploring, studying the culture, healing the Earth of trauma brought on by irresponsible mining or researching the history of Christianity over the past two thousand years. Some are in human guise, and some are in spirit form. Some look like what we call animals as they come from the species' home planet and interact with their fellow beings—those beings that we have labeled cats or cows or elephants. Some are brilliant cosmic mathematicians with a sense of humor; they are presently living here as penguins. Some are fledgling diplomats training for future postings on Earth when we have ET embassies here. In this book, these fascinating beings share their thoughts, origins and purposes for being here. 350 P. $14.95 ISBN 1-891824-28-7

⓬ EXPLORER RACE: Techniques for GENERATING SAFETY

Wouldn't you like to generate safety so you could go wherever you need to go and do whatever you need to do in a benevolent, safe and loving way for yourself? Learn safety as a radiated environment that will allow you to gently take the step into the new timeline, into a benevolent future and away from a negative past. 208 P. $9.95 ISBN 1-891824-26-0